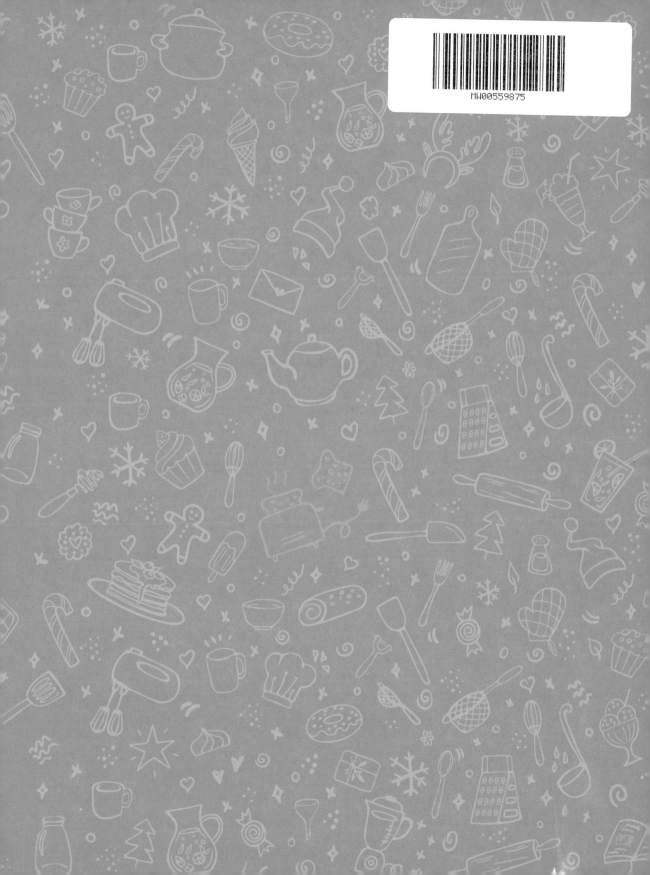

THE ELF ON THE SHELF®
FAMILY COOKBOOK

ALSO BY CHANDA A. BELL

Welcome!

THE ELF ON THE SHELF®
FAMILY
COOKBOOK

50 ELFtastic Recipes,
PLUS PLAYFUL ELF IDEAS, GAMES, ACTIVITIES, AND MORE!

CHANDA A. BELL

PHOTOGRAPHY BY GENYA O'NEALL

BASED ON
*THE ELF ON THE SHELF: A CHRISTMAS
TRADITION BY CHANDA A. BELL*

RECIPES CREATED BY
THERESA GAMBACORTA

WILLIAM MORROW
An Imprint of HarperCollinsPublishers

contents

Chapter 4:
SCOUT ELF DINNER TAKEOVER 123

Chapter 5:
CHRISTMAS AROUND THE WORLD 146

Chapter 6:
SCOUT ELF SPECIAL RETURNS 176

Hello there!

Ho H♥ Hello There!

A LETTER FROM SANTA CLAUS

What a joy to find you here! The inspiration for this cookbook came from millions of Scout Elf reports. My Scout Elves told me when families connect in their kitchens, tinker with ingredients, stir, mix, and pour their hearts into delicious festive foods, Christmas cheer swirls and twirls in the air!

"Imagine the Christmas cheer we'll spread when I ask my Scout Elf friends to share their favorite North Pole recipes, treats, and activities with families this Christmas season!" I said excitedly to Mrs. Claus. And before I could say, "Pass a piece of peppermint bark, please" she enlisted her Sweet Shop Elves—Toffee Tinselton, Ginger Jingleboots, Dash O'Jolly, and Pickles McCheer—to assist me. I sent them on a magical kitchen mission to fill your home with the season's most enticing crispy, shiny, melty, crunchy, gummy, savory, cheesy, bubbly, fresh, and fruity ingredients and share Sweet Shop Secrets to set the scene for holiday memories with your Scout Elves!

By the time your Scout Elves arrive this year, they'll be ready to use their elftastic skills, tools, and wit to take you on a magic-filled, delightful, and delicious holiday baking and cooking journey. But it wouldn't be possible without the faith, hope, and love of Santa's most fantastic helper—YOU! Wishing you a very Merry Christmas.

Yours truly,

Santa

Santa's GPS

(GOODIES PLANNING SYSTEM): NAVIGATING THIS BOOK

→ The Scout Elf games, puzzles, notecards, and special machines in this book are available as free downloadable pages that you can print at home from Santa's Official North Pole Blog (elfontheshelf .com/blog/cookbook).

Look out for Sweet Shop Secrets—little bits of insight, food facts, and ideas that will help you make Christmas magic with your Scout Elf friends!

Your journey begins with Scout Elf Return Week, winds through the Christmas season's beloved baked treats, cookies, movie-night snacks, and Santa-stopping goodies from my Scout Elves around the world, and then arrives at winter-warming elf-size eats. Your Scout Elves must depart and follow my sleigh back to the North Pole on December 24, but with my jolly permission, they'll return to share special celebration treats too! As you read—and cook!—keep watch for the following ways my Scout Elves invite you to celebrate the season's spirit that fuels Christmas magic.

- Your family may discover that your Scout Elves set out ingredients, a recipe, or a message card for a treat they'd love for you to make!
- Treats of all sizes might magically appear in your kitchen—the Scout Elves made them and will share the recipe, and how they did it!
- Scout Elves suggest North Pole recipes and projects for families to do together—and your Scout Elves may create a surprise with your finished treats!

Whether you're brand new to The Elf on the Shelf tradition or are looking for ways to include new, heartwarming ones, Christmas cheer is here! And my Scout Elves will lead the way!

Can you guess why they call me "Pickles"?

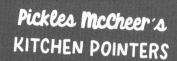

Pickles McCheer's
KITCHEN POINTERS

Read these guidelines first—and create a safe
and cheery kitchen!

- Read the recipe through to make sure you have all the ingredients and equipment you need.

- Before cooking and baking, always thoroughly wash your hands with warm, soapy water, then dry them with a towel!

- Tie back long hair and remove rings and bracelets—your hands are the best kitchen tools, and you don't want dough, melted chocolate, or raw ingredients sticking to jewelry.

- When needed to protect your clothing and hands, wear a festive apron and oven mitts—Mrs. Claus designs the kitchen gear we wear over our onesies!

- Use a sturdy step stool to reach high places—leave the climbing, swinging, and grappling to Scout Elf friends!

- To avoid slips, clean spills as you go—keep your workspace as tidy as the reindeer stalls.

- Always ask an adult for help with moving, lifting, and using home kitchen equipment and sharp tools.

- Use a timer to remind you when to check on items in the oven or on the stove—we call ours a "jingle bell."

- Be patient and wait for hot items to cool down before touching or tasting—you don't want to have to dip your tongue in a pile of snow!

ESSENTIAL
TOOLS

BIBS, BOBS, AND EXTRAS:

drinking straws, toothpicks, decorating ribbon, baker's twine, double-sided tape, ice-pop molds and/or sticks, decorative skewer sticks, mason jars (all sizes), a festive apron, number stickers, card stock, and any holiday wrapping paper, buttons, and bibs 'n' bobs you may find in your kitchen drawers for decorating an elf-vention.

Just as Scout Elves use tools to jump high, climb fast, glide gracefully, and swing easily, we bring you these essential tools to whip up the elftastic recipes in this book like a seasoned Christmas pro!

- Christmas and holiday cookie cutters, 1½ to 3½ inches
- Dry measuring cups
- Kitchen towels
- Large cutting board
- Liquid measuring cup
- Measuring spoons
- Mixing and prep bowls

- Nonstick skillets
- Oven mitts
- Parchment paper
- Pastry bags (12-inch preferred) and decorating tips or plastic zip-top bags
- Pastry brushes and food-safe decorating brushes
- Rolling pin
- Saucepans
- Sheet pans
- Sieve
- Silicone spatula
- Soup pot
- Tongs
- Wire cooling rack
- Wooden spoons

CHRISTMAS
MAGIC PANTRY PICKS

With Santa and Mrs. Claus' help, we used Christmas magic to pick out and deliver these baking staples, pantry sweets, and fridge and freezer foods to your home. Here's what you can expect to have on hand (and what your Scout Elves might get their tiny hands on).

PANTRY STAPLES

- All-purpose flour
- Baking powder
- Baking soda
- Bittersweet chocolate baking bar
- Brown sugar, dark and light
- Cinnamon— for baking, and in case of elftastrophes! (see page 199)
- Cooking spray
- Cornstarch
- Cream of tartar
- Dry whole milk powder

- Freshly ground black pepper
- Fruit jams, marmalades, butters, or curds
- Gel icing, for drawing, all colors
- Gel-based food coloring
- Granulated sugar
- Kosher salt
- Light corn syrup
- Luster dust
- Meringue powder
- Olive oil
- Peppermint extract

- Powdered sugar (confectioners' sugar)
- Pure maple syrup
- Pure vanilla extract, and clear vanilla extract, for decorating
- Spices, such as pumpkin pie mix, gingerbread mix, clove, allspice, and ginger
- Sweetened condensed milk
- Unsweetened cocoa powder
- White chocolate baking bar

BAKING AND DECORATING TREATS

- Assorted holiday cookies, such as sugar, pirouette, gingerbread, Chessmen, and Milano, for a "Santa, Stop Here!" Trifle (page 167)

- Baking chips, such as butterscotch, chocolate, white chocolate, peanut butter, and hot cocoa flavored

- Candy canes and starlight mints

- Chex cereal—rice, corn, or chocolate

- Chocolate and colored candy melts (also called candy wafers)

- Edible glitter

- Festive sprinkles, all colors, shapes, and themes, such as snowflakes and gold stars

- Kellogg's The Elf on the Shelf Sugar Cookie cereal

- Marshmallows—jumbo, standard, mini, and cream

- Sanding sugar, assorted colors

- Sweet Shop candies, including licorice laces, gumdrops, nonpareils (tiny, ball-shaped sprinkles), mini candy bars, candy-coated chocolates, candy eyeballs, jelly beans, toffee bits, sour candy—and lots of other shiny, tiny, glorious goodies for baking and decorating

THE ELF ON THE SHELF FAMILY COOKBOOK

HOW TO USE LUSTER DUST

Luster dust is a fine, flavorless edible powder that comes in an array of dazzling colors to add shimmer and shine to confections or for making Golden Cheer (page 25).

BRUSH: Place ¼ to ½ teaspoon luster dust in a bowl. Dip a dry bristled pastry brush into the powder. Tap to remove the excess, then use as directed.

PAINT: Place ½ teaspoon luster dust in a bowl. Stir in 1 to 2 drops of clear vanilla extract until the mixture has a creamy consistency. Paint it onto your surface. When finished, rest the brush on the edge of the bowl; when dry, the dust will flake off, and you can reuse it!

COUNTERTOP, FRIDGE, AND FREEZER FOODS

- Bananas
- Berries, such as strawberries, blueberries, and blackberries
- Buttermilk
- Cantaloupe
- Cheese, such as Cheddar and Monterey Jack, shredded, grated, and block
- Cherries and cranberries, frozen
- Clementines or navel oranges
- Cream cheese
- Eggs, large
- Green grapes
- Heavy cream
- Honeydew melon
- Kiwi

- Milk, whole
- Pineapple
- Puff pastry sheets, frozen
- Ready-to-bake cookie dough, such as chocolate chip or sugar
- Ready-to-bake pizza dough balls
- Shredded coconut
- Star fruit (also called carambola)
- Unsalted butter
- Unsweetened coconut milk beverage
- Vegetables, such as cherry tomatoes and spinach leaves
- Watermelon
- Whipped topping
- Yogurt

Mrs. Claus' sweet secrets:

VANILLA BUTTERCREAM BLISS FROSTING AND ROYAL ICING

Mrs. Claus is a smart cookie! She's an extraordinary designer and baker whose Sweet Shop treats are North Pole famous. Here are her secret recipes for making the creamiest buttercream frosting and thick royal icing for sugar cookie decorating and for constructing The Sweetest Shop (page 148).

Sweet secrets!

Mrs. Claus'
VANILLA BUTTERCREAM
BLISS FROSTING

MAKES ABOUT 4 CUPS

- ☐ ½ pound (2 sticks) unsalted butter, at room temperature
- ☐ Pinch of kosher salt
- ☐ 1 teaspoon pure vanilla extract
- ☐ 5 cups powdered sugar
- ☐ ½ cup whole milk or heavy cream, plus more as needed

1. In the bowl of a stand mixer fitted with the paddle attachment (or a large bowl, if using a handheld mixer), beat the butter and salt on medium-high speed until light and creamy-smooth, about 5 minutes. Add the vanilla and beat until incorporated.

2. Add 3 cups of the powdered sugar, then mix on low speed to combine, stopping to scrape down the sides of the bowl as needed. Add the milk, increase the speed to medium-high, and beat for 1 minute. Reduce the speed to low and add the remaining 2 cups powdered sugar, mixing until incorporated. If the consistency is too thick, add a bit more milk, 1 tablespoon at a time, and beat until spreadable, about 3 minutes.

3. Use the frosting immediately or transfer to an airtight container. Press a piece of plastic wrap against the top, then cover with the lid. Store in the refrigerator for up to 2 weeks.

CHOCOLATE BUTTERCREAM: Sift ½ cup unsweetened cocoa powder into the powdered sugar.

PEPPERMINT BUTTERCREAM: Swap the vanilla extract for peppermint extract.

STRAWBERRY BUTTERCREAM: Add ½ cup strawberry jam to the butter mixture in step 1.

COLORFUL BUTTERCREAM: Use a silicone spatula to gently fold 1 drop of gel-based food coloring into the finished buttercream—like us, a little goes a long way!

Mrs. Claus'
ROYAL ICING

MAKES ABOUT 6 CUPS

- ☐ 7 cups powdered sugar, plus more as needed
- ☐ 5 tablespoons meringue powder
- ☐ 1 teaspoon clear vanilla extract

1. Sift the powdered sugar into the bowl of a stand mixer fitted with the whisk attachment (or a large bowl, if using a handheld mixer). Sift the meringue powder into the bowl.

2. Add the vanilla and ¾ cup water and whisk on low speed to combine. Increase the speed to medium-high and continue whisking, stopping to scrape down the side of the bowl as needed, until thick and fluffy, 5 to 7 minutes. If the consistency is too thin, add more powdered sugar, 1 tablespoon at a time, to thicken. If the consistency is too thick, add more water, ½ teaspoon at a time, to loosen.

3. Use the icing immediately or transfer to an airtight container and cover with the lid. Store in the refrigerator for up to 2 weeks.

SWEET SHOP SECRET

Royal icing should have the thick consistency of toothpaste (but it's a lot tastier!). Use this icing for making outlines on decorating cookies and for constructing and attaching goodies to The Sweetest Shop (page 148).

After preparing the icing, separate a small amount and add 1 to 2 drops of water, until the icing has the consistency of honey. You can leave it snowy white or tint it with gel-based food coloring! Use this thinner icing for "flooding" (filling in) the shape. Use a toothpick to gently drag the icing to the edges for a smooth surface.

SUGAR COOKIE DECORATING TIPS

Mrs. Claus always says imagination and playfulness are the secrets to decorating beautiful sugar cookie cutouts that put a twinkle in Santa's eye! Your Scout Elves will even show you how to host a Sugar Cookie Decorating Party (page 64).

- **PASTRY BAGS:** We recommend using 12-inch pastry bags, which are just the right size for small hands to manage. Their conical shape makes them easy to maneuver, and you can fit them with various tips for control and decorating precision. You can use cloth or disposable bags. (Alternatively, you can fill plastic zip-top bags, snipping the tip off for the icing to flow.)

- **PASTRY TIPS:** These tips come in lots of different sizes and openings. We use small (2 mm) round tips for outlining cookies and large (3 mm) round tips for "flooding" icing, which means filling in the shape with a smooth, even layer of icing on the cookie's surface. Let the icing dry slightly (a few seconds) before adding sprinkles, sanding sugar, or candies. Wait for the icing to dry completely before adding creative touches, such as drawings or writing. We also use open star tips (12 to 18 mm) for piping meringues and swirling buttercream frosting.

- **TO FILL A PASTRY BAG:** Place an empty pastry bag in a tall glass, fold down the sides, use a silicone spatula, and fill no more than halfway with icing (refill as needed). You can also use this method for filling pastry bags with buttercream, meringue, and doughnut batter.

merry
MEASURING

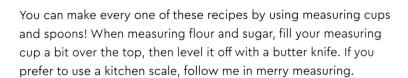

You can make every one of these recipes by using measuring cups and spoons! When measuring flour and sugar, fill your measuring cup a bit over the top, then level it off with a butter knife. If you prefer to use a kitchen scale, follow me in merry measuring.

FLOUR

- 1 cup / 120 g
- ½ cup / 60 g
- ⅓ cup / 40 g
- ¼ cup / 30 g

BUTTER

- ½ pound / 2 sticks / 227 g
- 12 tablespoons / 1½ sticks / 170 g
- 8 tablespoons / 1 stick / 113 g
- 4 tablespoons / ½ stick / 57 g

SUGAR

- 1 cup / 200 g
- ½ cup / 100 g
- ⅓ cup / 67 g
- ¼ cup / 50 g

THE ELF ON THE SHELF FAMILY COOKBOOK

JOLLY
JARGON

Here are some of the cooking terms you'll elf-counter in this book!

- **BAKE**: Cook in an oven
- **BLEND**: Mix thoroughly until smooth, often using a blender or food processor
- **BOIL**: Heat a liquid until it bubbles and steams
- **CHOP**: Cut food into smaller pieces
- **DICE**: Cut food into little cubes
- **MEASURE**: Use cups or spoons to get the right amounts of ingredients
- **MINCE**: Cut food into tiny bits
- **MIX**: Stir ingredients together
- **PEEL**: Remove the outer layer of fruits or vegetables
- **A PINCH**: ⅛ teaspoon
- **PIT OR SEED**: Remove pits or seeds from fruits or vegetables
- **POUR**: Transfer liquid from one container to another
- **SIMMER**: Cook gently, at a very low boil
- **TOSS**: Mix gently, usually to coat or cover
- **WHISK**: Beat ingredients rapidly to mix them or add air

What's cookin'?

TOFFEE TINSELTON'S
HOW-TOS

At Mrs. Claus' Sweet Shop, we crack, whisk, sift, line, fold, and roll our way to Christmas! Here's how we get the job done.

HOW TO CRACK AN EGG

Hold an egg in your hand over a bowl and lightly tap it on the edge to crack. Push your thumbs into the crack, pull the egg apart, and let the yolk and white fall into the bowl. Crack eggs into a separate bowl before adding them to your recipe—if a shell falls in, you can easily remove it before adding the egg to other ingredients.

HOW TO SEPARATE AN EGG

Set out two bowls. Hold the egg over one of the bowls and crack it. As you pull the egg apart, tip the yolk into one half of the shell, allowing the egg white to drop into the bowl. Tip the yolk back into the other half of the shell and repeat. Let the yolk drop into the other bowl.

HOW TO SIFT

Set a fine-mesh sieve over a bowl. Use a spoon to add ingredients slowly. Lift the sieve a bit and gently shake. Break apart lumps!

HOW TO WHISK

Hold the whisk in your hand, tilt the bowl toward you, and slowly move the whisk in circles to combine dry ingredients. Move the whisk faster to combine wet ingredients.

HOW TO LINE PANS

Grease a sheet pan with cooking spray to help parchment paper stick! To line an 8 × 8-inch or 9 × 13-inch baking pan with a handy overhang, place it on a sheet of parchment paper and cut the paper 2 inches larger than your pan. Spray the pan, press the paper in, then spray the paper.

HOW TO FOLD IN INGREDIENTS

Folding is a gentle mixing, so you don't deflate a light batter, and a silicone spatula is the best tool to use. Slowly pull ingredients from the edge of the bowl into the center and then up the middle. Repeat until combined.

HOW TO ROLL OUT COOKIE OR PASTRY DOUGH

To prevent sticky dough, work on a lightly floured surface. (Adding a bit of flour to the roller helps too!) To roll, gently press down on the rolling pin and roll the dough away from you once. Rotate the dough and roll away from you again, repeating until you have the desired thickness.

HOW TO PEEK FOR PEAKS!

Whisking egg whites or heavy cream "until peaks form" means until they hold a shape. Soft peaks (a fluffy mound), medium-firm peaks (a mound with stiff tips), or firm peaks—the tips of the mound will be thick and glossy and will stand straight up!

SCOUT ELF
SEEK-AND-FIND

Turn the pages for a festive quest to spot these special items and merry mischief in Scout Elf scenes!

A dinosaur

3 pretzel reindeer

A Scout Elf wearing a scarf with snowflakes on it

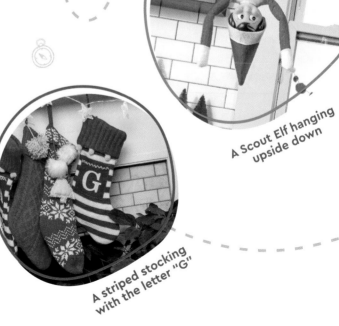

A Scout Elf hanging upside down

A striped stocking with the letter "G"

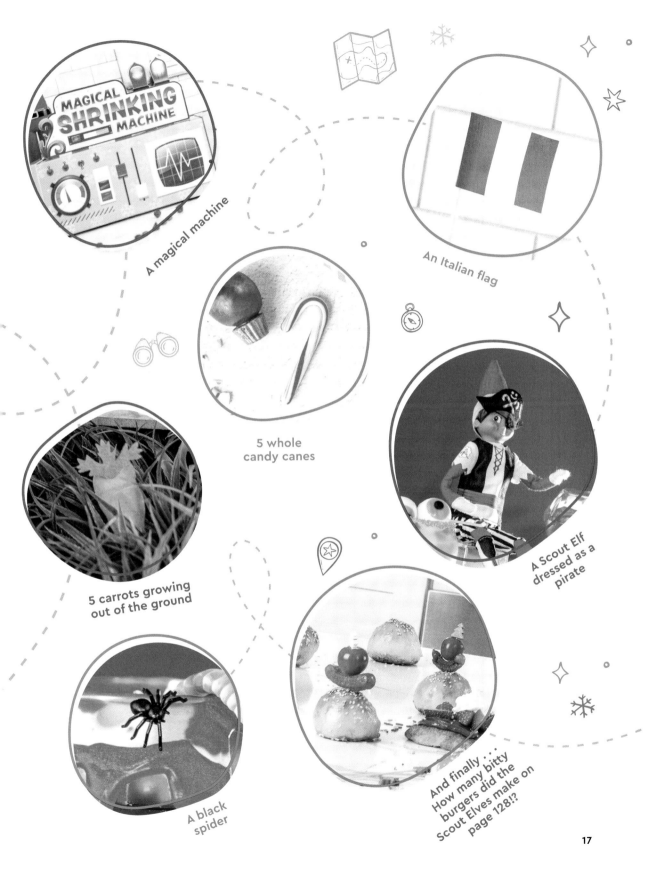

A magical machine

An Italian flag

5 whole
candy canes

5 carrots growing
out of the ground

A Scout Elf
dressed as a
pirate

A black
spider

And finally . . .
How many bitty
burgers did the
Scout Elves make on
page 128!?

By the time you read this message that you're holding in your hand,
We've surely made our way to you by sea, or air, or land.
Perhaps there was a magic door that opened—there we were!
We've brought our playful, merry hearts to bake, mix, pour, and stir!

Have you dreamt of Bacon Candy?
Doughnuts tossed in "snow"?
We have, of course—you'll find 'em here!—plus mugs of hot cocoa.
There are North Pole breakfast foods you love and lots of fun and laughter.
Don't delay! Let's turn the page and check out our first chapter!

Hooray for *Scout Elf Return Week!* Let's count down to Christmas Day.

FOR MORE INFORMATION ABOUT SCOUT ELF RETURN WEEK, VISIT ELFONTHESHELF.COM/SCOUT -ELF-RETURN-WEEK.

north Pole
NAME GENERATOR

To activate my magic when I first come to your home,
Just choose a name that's fit for me and I can call my own!
Once my name is chosen, you can jot it down right here:

_____

I'm looking forward to each day and bringing Christmas cheer!

FIND THE FIRST LETTER OF YOUR FIRST NAME . . .

A – Butter	H – Zart	O – Scout	V – Fizby
B - Winter	I - Marshmallow	P – Ginger	W – Jingle
C - Frosty	J – Sprinkle	Q – Cocoa	X – Nutmeg
D – Peppermint	K – Zesty	R - Cookie	Y – Cinnamon
E - Bingo	L - Martin	S – Toffee	Z – Sugar
F – Flurry	M – Skeeter	T – Starry	
G – Sweetie	N – Flip	U - Snowball	

THE ELF ON THE SHELF FAMILY COOKBOOK

AND THEN FIND THE FIRST LETTER OF THE STREET YOU LIVE ON . . .

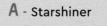
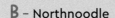

A - Starshiner

B – Northnoodle

C - O'Jolly

D – Dustlusterson

E - Tinselton

F – Von Snowington

G – Blitzen

H – Carolfield

I - Mac'Cooker

J – Jingleboots

K – McCheer

L - O'Cruncher

M – O'Lolly

N - Sprinkleton

O – Giftenville

P – Holidayson

Q - Stockingham

R - Trimmingworth

S - Yuleson

T - Snowberg

U – Frostington

V - Whirlingsworth

W – Twirlingsbridge

X - Leapington

Y – Von Cocoaville

Z – Scoutson

The Cheer Is Here!

PANCAKES

MAKES ABOUT 16 PANCAKES

Scout Elves have scaled more than 1 gazillion 327 Christmas trees, but we'll go out on a limb and say this pancake tree stacks up against all others as the merriest. See our taste-sational recipes for Golden Cheer (page 25) and other toppings to make your stack sparkly sweet and full of joy from tip to trunk!

FOR THE PANCAKES
- ☐ 2 cups all-purpose flour
- ☐ 1½ teaspoons baking powder
- ☐ 1½ teaspoons baking soda
- ☐ 2 tablespoons granulated sugar
- ☐ ¼ teaspoon kosher salt
- ☐ 2 large eggs
- ☐ 3 tablespoons unsalted butter, melted
- ☐ 1 teaspoon pure vanilla extract
- ☐ 2 cups buttermilk
- ☐ 1 to 2 drops green gel-based food coloring (the more the greener)
- ☐ ¼ cup Golden Cheer (recipe follows)
- ☐ 1 large raspberry for the Christmas "star," plus more raspberries, for serving

1. Make the pancakes: In a large bowl, whisk together the flour, baking powder, baking soda, granulated sugar, and salt.
2. In a medium bowl, whisk together the eggs. Add the butter, vanilla, and buttermilk and whisk to combine.
3. Add the egg mixture to the bowl with the flour mixture and whisk to make a smooth batter. Add a drop of green food coloring and mix it in, adding a second drop if you prefer a greener mixture. Transfer the batter to the refrigerator to rest for 15 minutes to activate fluffiness!
4. Preheat the griddle to 350°F or heat the nonstick skillet or griddle over medium heat.
5. Working in batches, spoon about ½ cup of the batter onto the griddle, forming a large pancake about 6 inches wide. Cook until bubbles form on the surface of the pancake, 1 to 2 minutes. Flip and cook 1 to 2 minutes longer, or until the second side is lightly browned. Transfer the pancake to a plate and cover with aluminum foil to keep warm. Continue cooking, forming more pancakes, each smaller and smaller in size—they will need less cooking time—until you have used up all your batter.
6. Make the Maple Snow Glaze: In a small bowl, whisk together the butter, powdered sugar, maple syrup, milk, and vanilla until smooth. Set aside.
7. To assemble the Christmas tree: Stack the pancakes on the festive plate from largest to smallest. Drizzle some of the Maple Snow Glaze over the top and down the sides, reserving the rest for dipping. (Alternatively, pour on your favorite pancake syrup.) Sprinkle the pancake "tree" with Golden Cheer and top with the raspberry "star." Serve with raspberries.

FOR THE MAPLE SNOW GLAZE
MAKES ABOUT 1 CUP

- ☐ 4 tablespoons (½ stick) unsalted butter, melted
- ☐ 1½ cups powdered sugar
- ☐ 1 tablespoon pure maple syrup
- ☐ ¼ cup whole milk
- ☐ 1 teaspoon pure vanilla extract

SPECIAL EQUIPMENT

Electric griddle or nonstick skillet or griddle

Festive serving plate

SWEET SHOP SECRET

Make elf-size pancakes for your Scout Elves! Drop pancake batter onto the griddle by the ¼ teaspoon. (Alternatively, you can fill a plastic zip-top bag halfway with batter and snip off a corner for the batter to flow.) Cook until small bubbles form on the surface of the pancakes, about 20 seconds. Flip and continue cooking until golden brown, about 20 seconds more.

Yummy!

GOLDEN CHEER

MAKES ABOUT 1 CUP

- ☐ 4 undecorated Bright Light Sugar Cookies (page 60) or plain bakery-style store-bought sugar cookies, broken into smaller pieces (see Sweet Shop Secret below)
- ☐ ¼ cup powdered sugar
- ☐ 1½ teaspoons gold luster dust

SWEET SHOP SECRET

To easily crush hard ingredients such as candies, nuts, chips, pretzels, graham crackers, or cereal, place them in a zip-top bag, press out most of the air, and seal closed. Using a rolling pin, roll back and forth across the bag, crushing the ingredients as elf size as you like.

Flip! Flip! Hooray!
PANCAKE SWIRLS AND TOPPINGS

Raisin' Christmas spirit is our specialty, and so is adding sweet 'n' salty flavors to elf-evate your North Pole pancakes. For these stacks, omit the green food coloring in the batter— and swirl, flip, and top away!

GINGERBREAD STACK: In a small bowl, whisk together 4 tablespoons (½ stick) melted butter, ¼ cup packed light brown sugar, ¼ cup dark molasses, 2½ teaspoons gingerbread spice mix, and ½ teaspoon vanilla extract until smooth. Gently swirl the mixture into the pancake batter before cooking. Top with whipped cream and garnish with sprinkles, raisins, or mini gingerbread cookies.

IMPERIAL CEREAL CAKES: Stir 1 cup crushed The Elf on the Shelf cereal (any flavor!) into the pancake batter before cooking. Top with chocolate sauce, pure maple syrup, or whipped cream, plus ¼ cup more cereal.

NUTS FOR BACON: Stir ½ cup cooked, crumbled bacon into the pancake batter before cooking. Top with maple syrup and ¼ cup crushed nuts, such as Mexican Hot Chocolate Candied Nuts (page 164).

CINNAMON SWIRL: In a small bowl, whisk together 4 tablespoons (½ cup) melted butter, ¼ cup packed light brown sugar, and 2 teaspoons ground cinnamon until smooth. Gently swirl the mixture into the pancake batter before cooking. Top with pats of butter, maple syrup and raisins, or cinnamon candies.

PEPPERMINT CANDY CAKES: Stir 1 teaspoon peppermint extract and ½ cup crushed candy canes into the pancake batter before cooking. Top with whipped cream and ¼ cup more crushed candy canes or red and white sprinkles.

STICKY BANANAS: Melt 2 tablespoons butter in a pan, add ¼ cup packed light brown sugar, and stir to melt the sugar. Add 1 cup ½-inch-thick banana "coins" (from about 1½ bananas) in a single layer and cook until the bottoms of the coins are browned and sticky, about 2 minutes. Flip and cook about 2 minutes more. Spoon the bananas over the pancakes.

THE ELF ON THE SHELF FAMILY COOKBOOK

GOLDEN CHEER

Place the cookies, powdered sugar, and luster dust in the bowl of a food processor and blend into a fine, dustlike consistency that shimmers–the cheer is here! Store in an airtight container at room temperature for up to 1 week.

Uh-Oh!!

D'EGGRATIONS

MAKES 2 DOZEN EGG BITES

While you were fast asleep, we got crackin' and did something near and dear to our hearts—d'eggorated! We started by making eggs'cellent ornaments for your breakfast table.

- ☐ Cooking spray
- ☐ ½ cup minced cooked ham or salami
- ☐ ½ cup minced red bell pepper
- ☐ ½ cup minced green bell pepper
- ☐ ½ cup minced red onions
- ☐ 1 cup packed baby spinach leaves
- ☐ 6 large eggs
- ☐ ¼ cup whole milk
- ☐ ¼ teaspoon kosher salt
- ☐ Pinch of freshly ground black pepper
- ☐ 2 tablespoons grated Parmesan cheese

SPECIAL EQUIPMENT

Two 12-cup mini muffin tins, or one 24-cup mini muffin tin

1. Position two oven racks, evenly spaced, in the center of the oven. Preheat the oven to 350°F. Grease the muffin tin cups with cooking spray.
2. Distribute the bits of meat evenly among the muffin tin cups.
3. In a medium skillet over medium heat, cook the peppers and onions until the peppers are soft and the onions are translucent, about 3 minutes. Add the spinach and stir until wilted, about 30 seconds. Remove from the heat.
4. Using a teaspoon, distribute the cooked vegetables evenly among the muffin tin cups. Press down with the back of the spoon.
5. Crack the eggs into a large bowl and whisk until well beaten. Add the milk, salt, and pepper and whisk to combine. Transfer the egg mixture to a measuring cup for easier pouring, then pour the egg batter into the muffin tin cups, filling just to the top. Sprinkle the tops with the cheese.
6. Bake until the eggs puff and are set in the center, about 10 minutes. Cool on a wire rack for 10 minutes, then use a butter knife to gently loosen them from the pan. Listen for an egg-splosion of yum when you pop one in your mouth!

SWEET SHOP SECRET

Eggs'periment

Vegetables, like Christmas ornaments, come in festive colors! Swap the peppers and onions for minced zucchini, broccoli, mushrooms, and/or chopped fresh herbs, such as parsley, chives, or basil, to make singularly sp'eggtacular bites.

→ Download printable notecard at elfontheshelf.com/blog/cookbook.

Bacon CANDY

I have a plan that's spiff and dandy.
Here's the bacon (and the candy)!
A wish come true? There's no mistakin':
Drizzle candy on your bacon!
Crispy, spiced, and salty-sweet,
Bacon? Candy? Did you meet?
For bacon's sake, a true delight,
Step right up and take a bite!

- ¼ cup packed dark brown sugar
- 1 teaspoon ground cinnamon
- 1 pound thick-cut bacon strips
- One 4.4-ounce white chocolate baking bar, chopped
- 2 teaspoons coconut oil
- One 4.4-ounce bittersweet chocolate baking bar, chopped

SPECIAL EQUIPMENT
Festive serving plate

1. Preheat the oven to 375°F. Line a sheet pan with aluminum foil.
2. In a small bowl, use a fork to combine the brown sugar and cinnamon.
3. Place the bacon strips side by side on the prepared sheet pan, sprinkle the cinnamon sugar from top to bottom, and use your fingers to rub it in. Repeat on the other side. Twist each strip into a "candy" spiral, using your pointer finger as a guide by wrapping and then pulling.
4. Bake until the sugar bubbles and the bacon is crispy, 15 to 20 minutes. Use tongs to stack the spirals on the festive serving plate.
5. Combine the white chocolate and 1 teaspoon of the coconut oil in a small microwave-safe bowl. Heat, uncovered, on high, in 30-second increments, stirring in between, until melted and smooth, about 2 minutes total. Repeat the process in a separate bowl with the bittersweet chocolate and the remaining 1 teaspoon oil. Drizzle some of the white chocolate over the bacon, followed by some of the bittersweet chocolate, reserving any remaining chocolates for dipping!

Sn❄wy SMOOTHIE

MAKES TWO 8-OUNCE SMOOTHIES

The snow at the North Pole is a natural comedian; it falls from the sky with impeccable timing, delivers "slip 'n' slide" gags, and keeps us Scout Elves rolling in laughter. But the snowpeople? They're chill. So is our recipe for a frosty, fun, snowy smoothie—s'now doubt you'll love it too!

- ☐ Honey
- ☐ 1 tablespoon edible blue glitter or luster dust, plus more for garnish
- ☐ 1½ cups unsweetened coconut milk beverage
- ☐ 1 small banana, cut into chunks
- ☐ ½ teaspoon pure vanilla extract
- ☐ 2 tablespoons unsweetened finely shredded coconut, plus more for garnish
- ☐ 2 ice cubes
- ☐ Whipped topping

SPECIAL EQUIPMENT
Two 10-ounce glasses
Blender

1. Use a butter knife to spread a thin coating of honey on the rim and 1 inch around the top of the outside of the glasses. Coat the rims and sides of the glasses with glitter.
2. In the blender, combine the coconut milk, banana, vanilla, coconut, and ice cubes and blend on high until smooth and frothy.
3. Divide the smoothie between the glasses, top with a snowy mountain of whipped topping, and garnish with a little more coconut and glitter—snow nice!

24 DAYS OF ADVENT'ROUS CHEER

This Advent'rous calendar counts down the days till Christmas, from December 1 through our departure on Christmas Eve, December 24, and includes some of the surprises and recipes that we planned to share. Follow along each day or pick and choose as you wish!

1 We set the scene for a welcome-back breakfast with D'eggorations (page 27) and festive decorations!

2 Yule Love This Log (page 000) for your tree trimming.

3 Discover Santa's top-secret all-time-favorite cookie recipe (page 47)!

4 Enjoy reading a Christmas storybook, such as *The Elf on the Shelf: A Christmas Tradition*, with a Mug'nificent Cocoa (page 42).

5 Bake Shimmering S'nownuts (page 51) and dust with sugar, or glaze and decorate.

6 Deck the halls, then Meat Us at the Wreath (page 69).

7 Host a Sugar Cookie Decorating Party (page 64).

8 Design The Sweetest Shop (page 148).

9 Watch an Elf Pets animated special for Merry Movie Night, and enjoy melty, munchy snacks (see chapter 3).

10 Play Carol Conundrum (page 78).

11 Host a Decked-Out Dippers (page 80) date.

12 Put us in charge of after-school snacks and savory surprises.

13 Did it snow? Make Snow Blizzard Cream (page 121).

14 We'll need more snowballs—STAT—for our Snowball Fight! (page 138).

15 Create Mug'nificent Toppers (page 42).

16 Play Christmas Carol Karaoke (page 79).

THE ELF ON THE SHELF FAMILY COOKBOOK

17
Bake A Party in a Pan Treat (page 77).

18
Design your own Christmas cards, address them, and sign our names too!

19
Thread Fa-La-Lollipops (page 90).

20
Bake a one-of-a-kind Everything but the Kitchen Sink Cookie (page 171) for Santa.

21
The reindeer are gearing up! Make Peanut Butter Pikku Deer Cookies (page 66) in honor of them.

22
Design gift tags for your presents!

Make a plate of Doughnut Delights for your elves (page 55).
23 ❓❗

24
We'll be following Santa's sleigh back to the North Pole tonight. Write us a good-bye letter—and we'll write you one too.

25
THE BIG DAY IS HERE—BECAUSE OF YOUR CHRISTMAS CHEER!

Adventure awaits!

Toy Bag
BREAKFAST BUNDLES

GRAB A bundle AND TRY a bite!

The contents of Santa's bag
of presents are a secret, but
here's a mini version filled with
scrumptious scrambled eggs and
sausage that's a cinch to make!

★ OUR MESSAGES GOT SCRAMBLED
WITH THE SAUSAGE AND EGGS—
NO YOLK, HELP!

1. aveH nuf mmingtri teh reet!
2. Cmashrist tspiri esmak teh deerrein yfl!
3. Sanat slove kmil wiht ish iescook.

1. Have fun trimming the tree!
2. Christmas spirit makes the reindeer fly!
3. Santa loves milk with his cookies.

- ☐ Cooking spray
- ☐ All-purpose flour
- ☐ One 16-ounce ball store-bought pizza dough, at room temperature
- ☐ ½ pound ground pork breakfast sausage
- ☐ 3 large eggs, lightly beaten
- ☐ ¼ teaspoon kosher salt
- ☐ Pinch of freshly ground black pepper
- ☐ ¼ cup shredded cheese, such as Cheddar

SPECIAL EQUIPMENT

12-cup muffin tin

Twelve 6- to 8-inch pieces of baker's twine

1. Position an oven rack in the center of the oven. Preheat the oven to 375°F. Grease the muffin tin cups with cooking spray.

2. Lightly flour a clean work surface and turn out the pizza dough. Using your clean hands, pinch off 12 equal-size pieces of dough (about 1¼ ounces each). Roll each portion into a soft ball, then use your fingers to flatten and stretch it into a round 3½ inches in diameter and set aside.

3. Warm a medium nonstick skillet over medium heat. Add the sausage and cook, breaking it up with a wooden spoon, until browned and cooked through (no pink parts!), about 5 minutes. Push the sausage to one side of the skillet and reduce the heat to low. Pour the eggs into the empty side of the skillet, season with the salt and pepper, and scramble until set, 1 to 2 minutes. Stir the sausage and eggs together, add the cheese, and continue cooking until the cheese is melted, about 30 seconds more. Remove from the heat.

4. Place about 2 tablespoons of the egg mixture in the center of each dough round. Fold the edges of the dough up and around the filling, then pinch them together, forming a small bundle. Tie each bundle closed with a piece of baker's twine, by crisscrossing, then gently pulling to secure it. Use your fingers to create a bow. Place each bundle in a muffin tin cup.

5. Bake until golden brown, 15 to 20 minutes. Cool slightly, then remove the bundles from the muffin tins before serving. Remove the twine before eating by breaking open the bundle at the top.

Christmas CRUNCHICLES

MAKES 6 FROZEN POPS

I thought it would be n'ice to surprise you with breakfast, but I arrived in a flurry on a chilly North Pole wind and your breakfast is now an icy treat. My clever plan was bungled but not my surprise! Behold, breakfast on a stick—sweet cereal crunchicles! A frosty delight just like we make them at the North Pole.

- ☐ ½ cup vanilla yogurt
- ☐ ½ cup whole milk
- ☐ ¼ teaspoon pure vanilla extract
- ☐ 1¼ cups Kellogg's The Elf on the Shelf Sugar Cookie cereal (or another favorite cereal)
- ☐ 1¼ cups sliced hulled strawberries

SPECIAL EQUIPMENT

6-well ice-pop mold (3.4 ounces each), with or without an ice-pop stick attachment

6 ice-pop sticks (optional)

1. In a medium bowl, whisk together the yogurt, milk, and vanilla. Add the cereal and strawberries and stir to combine.
2. Divide the mixture evenly among the 6 ice-pop molds, then insert the ice-pop sticks (if needed) into the center of each mold. Freeze the crunchicles until solid, about 4 hours.
3. Before serving, let the crunchicles sit at room temperature for 5 minutes for easy unmolding, or run the molds under warm water for 30 seconds to loosen.

Check the freezer for a yummy surprise!

Mrs. Claus' Santa-Size BATCH OF CoCOA MIX

MAKES ENOUGH MIX FOR ABOUT THIRTY 1-CUP SERVINGS

Mrs. Claus stores her homemade cocoa mix in a large glass jar and decorates it with a red velvet ribbon for the Big Man in Red. Here's her recipe for a batch that should last through *Scout Elf Return Week*. Use Mrs. Claus' Mix to make *Mug'nificent Cocoa* (page 42) and for *Scout Elf Cocoa Bombs* (page 106).

- ☐ 2½ cups unsweetened cocoa powder
- ☐ 2½ cups sugar
- ☐ 2 cups dry whole milk powder
- ☐ 1 teaspoon kosher salt

SPECIAL EQUIPMENT

32-ounce mason jar

Baker's twine or red velvet ribbon

Sift together the cocoa powder, sugar, milk powder, and salt over a large bowl. Discard any lumps that remain. Transfer the mixture to the mason jar and seal. Tie baker's twine or a red velvet ribbon around the mouth of the jar.

Loading Christmas Spirit...

Mug'nificent COCOA

- 3 heaping tablespoons Mrs. Claus' Santa-Size Batch of Cocoa Mix (page 40), or store-bought mix
- 2 tablespoons semisweet chocolate chips, or 2 to 3 mini chocolate candy bars, chopped
- 1½ cups boiling water
- Marshmallows
- Mug'nificent Toppers (optional)

Place the cocoa and chocolate in a large mug. Add the water and stir well. Top with marshmallows and, if using, whatever other toppers you wish!

SWEET SHOP SECRET
Mug'nificent Toppers
Use the picture as a guide to make these terrific toppers!

POLAR BEARS:

Use a spot of store-bought frosting or icing as "glue" to attach 1 standard marshmallow to a jumbo marshmallow for the polar bear head and body. Use a little more frosting or icing to attach 2 mini marshmallows for ears, candy eyeballs for eyes, and a brown candy-coated chocolate for a nose.

REINDEER:

Dip standard marshmallows in melted chocolate candy to coat. Break a thin pretzel in half and attach to the marshmallow to make antlers before the candy sets. Add candy eyeballs for eyes and a red candy-coated chocolate for a nose.

SNOWPEOPLE:

Use colored gel icing to draw eyes, a nose, and a mouth on top of a jumbo marshmallow. Or use a spot of store-bought frosting or icing as "glue" to attach a candy-corn nose.

Jolliest Boss Style

Peanut Butter Pizazz

Mexican Spice Is Nice

Golden Cheer Cocoa

I'll Have S'more

Whirlwind Cocoa

44

Mug'nificent Ways
TO COCOA

Gooey, JUMBO, mini, and fluff—
more marshmallows, please, it's not enough!
Golden Cheer and luster dust—
whipped cream mountains are a must.
Choc'o'late, cookies, sprinkles (so fly!)—
galore-ious toppings that touch the sky.
We're on a mission; there's no stopping
till we've Christmas-cheered your toppings.
Dip, whirl, sprinkle, shine—what's your favorite hot design?
Choco magic, a mug so 'nificent!
Which one first? A cocoa predicament!

WHIRLWIND COCOA: Combine peppermints or crushed candy canes, snowflake sprinkles, and blue luster dust. Sprinkle over whipped cream–topped cocoa for a snowy whirlwind effect. Looks like your cocoa got caught in our wind simulator that we use to train for Elf Return Week!

GOLDEN CHEER COCOA: Top cocoa with a mountain of whipped cream and sprinkle with Golden Cheer (page 25) for a cocoa that shines.

JOLLIEST BOSS STYLE: Make your cocoa in a Santa-size mug, leaving room for 2 jumbo marshmallows or a whole lotta mini marshmallows. Top with whipped cream, crushed peppermints, and chocolate chips.

I'LL HAVE S'MORE: Dip the rim of your empty mug in marshmallow cream, then crushed graham crackers. Make your cocoa, then cover the surface with marshmallows and drizzle with chocolate syrup.

PEANUT BUTTER PIZAZZ: Swap peanut butter chips or 2 peanut butter cups for the chocolate chips. Stir to melt, then top with whipped cream, drizzles of creamy peanut butter, and crushed salted peanuts.

MEXICAN SPICE IS NICE: Combine a pinch each of cinnamon, nutmeg, cayenne, and allspice to powdered cocoa mix. Top with whipped cream and shavings from a spicy hot chocolate bar.

45

Santa's Top-Secret
BREAKFAST C🍪🍪KIES

**MAKES ABOUT
1½ DOZEN COOKIES**

We know we're known for being a bit messy sometimes. But while we might spill milk or cocoa, we'd never spill secrets. So we asked and got permission to share the top-secret details of Santa's all-time favorite cookie with you! Santa keeps a jar of these ingredients ready to go for cookies on a moment's notice. Layer the ingredients and set them aside to bake up later, or pour into a bowl and bake them now!

- ¼ cup raisins or dried cranberries
- ¼ cup chocolate, peanut butter, or white chocolate chips
- 1½ cups old-fashioned rolled oats (not quick cooking)
- ¾ cup all-purpose flour
- ¼ teaspoon kosher salt
- ½ teaspoon baking soda
- ½ teaspoon ground cinnamon
- ¼ cup granulated sugar
- ½ cup packed dark brown sugar
- 8 tablespoons (1 stick) butter, at room temperature
- 1 large egg, at room temperature
- ½ teaspoon pure vanilla extract

SPECIAL EQUIPMENT
32-ounce mason jar

1. Place the raisins in the bottom of the jar, then add layers of the baking chips, oats, flour, salt, baking soda, cinnamon, granulated sugar, and brown sugar. Don't mix—keep the layers separate. Seal the jar and keep the top-secret mix on your counter for later—up to 2 weeks!
2. When you are ready to bake, line a sheet pan with parchment paper and set aside. Combine the butter, egg, and vanilla in a large bowl and mix with a wooden spoon until creamy.
3. Carefully tip and turn the jar over the bowl so that just the top layers of brown sugar and granulated sugar fall in (it's okay if a little of the flour falls in). Stir, and keep stirring, until the sugar is creamy and incorporated. Elftastic! Now tip and turn the jar over the bowl so that just the cinnamon, baking soda, salt, and flour fall in—it's okay if some of the oatmeal sneaks out. Keep stirring until they are mixed in. Scrape the sides of the bowl while mixing. Merry-velous!

(recipe continues on next page)

TOP SECRET TOP SECRET SECRET

4. Tip the final layers of oats, chips, and raisins into the bowl. Stir, and keep stirring, until well combined, and a strong, sturdy dough forms. Fab.

5. Using your clean hands or a cookie scoop, shape the dough into walnut-size balls, (about 1 tablespoon each) and place them 1 inch apart on the prepared sheet pan. Gently flatten them with your hand a bit. Refrigerate until firm, 20 to 30 minutes.

6. Preheat the oven to 350°F.

7. Transfer the cookies from the refrigerator to the oven and bake until the edges are golden brown, 8 to 10 minutes. Cool on the pan on a wire rack for 10 minutes, then transfer the cookies directly to the rack to cool completely. Store the cookies in an airtight container at room temperature for up to 1 week.

TOP SECRET

PROPERTY OF THE NORTH POLE

TOP SECRET

Cookie secrets are the sweetest!

➔ Download a Top Secret sign at elfontheshelf.com/blog/cookbook.

WE'VE RETURNED!

49

Shimmering S'NOWNUTS

The warm spices in our fave old-fashioned cake doughnut recipe will give your house the woodsy, warming scent of a North Pole pine grove–ah, "home sweet home." Pair them with Mug'nificent Cocoa (page 42) to make a winter's day feel oh so cozy. While these doughnuts are topped with shimmering "snow," you could dress them up instead with Snow Day Glaze (page 56). We "doughnut" know about you, but we think they're also great for zipping and zooming on a snowy winter night!

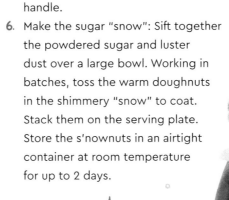

MAKES 1 DOZEN DOUGHNUTS

FOR THE DOUGHNUTS

- ☐ Cooking spray
- ☐ 2 cups all-purpose flour
- ☐ ½ cup granulated sugar
- ☐ 2 teaspoons baking powder
- ☐ ½ teaspoon kosher salt
- ☐ 1 tablespoon ground cinnamon or pumpkin pie spice
- ☐ ¾ cup buttermilk
- ☐ 2 large eggs
- ☐ 2 tablespoons unsalted butter, melted
- ☐ 2 teaspoons pure vanilla extract

FOR THE SUGAR "SNOW"

- ☐ 1 cup powdered sugar
- ☐ 1 teaspoon pearl white luster dust

SPECIAL EQUIPMENT

12-doughnut mold

Pastry bag fitted with a large round tip (see Mrs. Claus' Sugar Cookie Decorating Tips on page 11)

Toothpick

Festive serving plate

1. Preheat the oven to 375°F. Grease the doughnut mold with cooking spray.

2. Make the doughnuts: In a large bowl, whisk together the flour, granulated sugar, baking powder, salt, and cinnamon.

3. In a separate bowl, whisk to combine the buttermilk, eggs, butter, and vanilla. Gradually add the buttermilk mixture to the flour mixture, gently whisking between additions, until the batter is smooth.

4. Use a silicone spatula to fill the pastry bag no more than two-thirds full. Pipe the batter into the doughnut molds, filling each about three-quarters of the way. Refill the bag with the remaining batter and pipe the remaining doughnuts.

5. Bake until the toothpick inserted into a doughnut comes out clean, about 10 minutes. Cool on the pan on a wire rack for 5 minutes, then transfer the doughnuts directly to the rack until cool enough to handle.

6. Make the sugar "snow": Sift together the powdered sugar and luster dust over a large bowl. Working in batches, toss the warm doughnuts in the shimmery "snow" to coat. Stack them on the serving plate. Store the s'nownuts in an airtight container at room temperature for up to 2 days.

Elf-size

Teeny Tiny Sprinkles

DOUGHNUT DELIGHTS!

Press cereal "O"s onto a wet paper towel, then dip them in powdered sugar. Use a toothpick to clear the "doughnut" hole of excess sugar. Or you can dip the "O"s in Mrs. Claus' Royal Icing (page 10) or doughnut glaze (see page 56) and decorate them with festive sprinkles. Use these elf-size doughnuts to decorate the rim of a We ♥ You Strawberry Milkshake (page 194) or make a little plate of them for your Scout Elves.

Snow Day
GLAZED S'NOWNUTS

MAKES ABOUT 1½ CUPS GLAZE FOR 1 DOZEN DOUGHNUTS

Dip plain s'nownuts in vanilla or other flavored glazes, then top with goodies for a cakey circle celebration!

- 12 plain s'nownuts (see page 51)

FOR THE VANILLA GLAZE
- 3 cups powdered sugar, plus more as needed
- ¼ cup heavy cream or whole milk
- 1½ teaspoons light corn syrup
- ½ teaspoon pure vanilla extract
- ¼ cup hot water, plus more as needed

FOR DECORATING (OPTIONAL)
- Golden Cheer (page 25)
- The Elf on the Shelf cereal (any flavor)
- Festive sprinkles
- Crushed candy canes or starlight mints

1. Allow the s'nownuts to cool completely.
2. Make the glaze: Sift the powdered sugar into a large bowl. Add the cream, corn syrup, vanilla, and water and whisk until smooth and glossy. If it's still too thick, add a few drops more water to loosen. If it's too runny, add more powdered sugar 1 teaspoon at a time, to thicken.
3. Dip the s'nownuts in the glaze to coat the tops. Set the s'nownuts, glazed side up, on a wire cooling rack.
4. To decorate: Working quickly, before the glaze sets, sprinkle on any desired toppings.

CHOCOLATE GLAZE: Add ¼ cup unsweetened cocoa powder. Add 1 to 2 tablespoons more hot water as needed to achieve a glaze consistency.

PEPPERMINT GLAZE: Swap in peppermint extract for the vanilla extract.

MERRY AND BRIGHT GLAZES: Add a drop of gel-based food coloring to tint the vanilla glaze any color you wish!

Peppermint Glaze

Chocolate Glaze

Merry and Bright Glaze

Yummy
Sprinkles!

CHAPTER 2

DECK THE HALLS!

Bright Light SUGAR COOKIES

When Santa gave us our assignment to spread more Christmas cooking cheer this season, we asked Mrs. Claus for her favorite recipe for sugar cookie cutouts so we could bring it to you! You can form the dough into any shape you wish, but we think a cookie string of Christmas lights is a wonder-filled way to show Santa your cooking creativity!

FOR THE COOKIE DOUGH

- ☐ 2¾ cups all-purpose flour, plus more for dusting
- ☐ ½ teaspoon baking powder
- ☐ ¼ teaspoon kosher salt
- ☐ ½ pound (2 sticks) unsalted butter, at room temperature
- ☐ ¾ cup granulated sugar
- ☐ 1 large egg
- ☐ 1 teaspoon pure vanilla extract

FOR DECORATING

- ☐ 3 cups Mrs. Claus' Royal Icing (page 10)
- ☐ Gel-based food coloring (any color), for the lightbulb screw
- ☐ Sanding sugar, assorted colors

SPECIAL EQUIPMENT

3-inch Christmas lightbulb cookie cutters

Drinking straw

2 pastry bags—one fitted with a small round tip for outlining and one with a large round tip for "flooding" (see page 10)

Toothpick

Baker's twine, for stringing the cookies

Festive serving platter (optional)

1. Make the dough: In a large bowl, whisk together the flour, baking powder, and salt.

2. In the bowl of a stand mixer fitted with the paddle attachment (or another large bowl, if using a handheld mixer), beat the butter and sugar on medium speed until pale and fluffy, 3 to 5 minutes. Add the egg and vanilla, then mix on low speed until incorporated.

3. Add the flour mixture to the butter mixture and continue to mix on low speed for about 30 seconds. Stop and scrape down the sides of the bowl, then continue mixing until a dough forms, about 30 seconds more.

4. Divide the dough evenly into 2 balls. Wrap each ball in plastic wrap and shape it into a flat disk about ½ inch thick. Refrigerate for 1 hour.

5. Line 2 sheet pans with parchment paper. Lightly flour a work surface. Working with 1 disk at a time, roll it out to ¼ inch thick. Cut out shapes and transfer them to the prepared sheet pans, arranging them 1 inch apart. Use the straw to gently punch out a hole at the "screw" end of each cookie. Gather any dough scraps, pat them into a ball, roll out again, and cut out more shapes. Refrigerate the cutouts until firm, 20 to 30 minutes.

6. Position two oven racks, evenly spaced, in the center of the oven. Preheat the oven to 350°F.

7. Transfer the cookies from the refrigerator to the oven and bake, switching the pans on the oven racks halfway through, until the cookies are lightly browned around the edges, 10 to 12 minutes. Cool on the pan on a wire rack for 10 minutes, then transfer the cookies directly to the rack to cool completely before decorating.

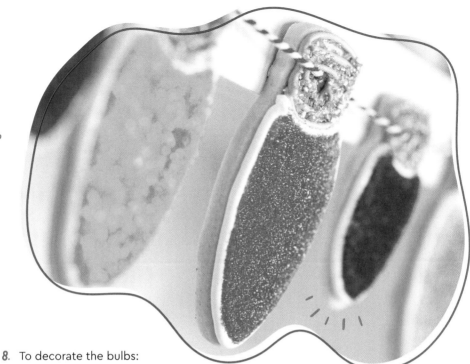

8. To decorate the bulbs:
   Fill the pastry bag fitted with the
   small tip with 1 cup icing and outline the
   bulbs, leaving the screw portion empty. Fill the pastry bag fitted with the
   larger tip with 1 cup more icing and "flood" (fill in) the bulbs. Let set slightly,
   then cover the bulbs with sanding sugar.

9. To decorate the screws: Place the remaining 1 cup icing in a medium bowl.
   Tint it with your choice of food coloring by dropping a small amount into
   the icing off the tip of the toothpick. Stir. Add more until your desired color
   is achieved. Fill a pastry bag with the colored icing and draw zigzag lines to
   create the screw, leaving the hole open. Let the icing dry completely.

10. String the cookies on the twine and hang them like garland anywhere—in
    a doorway, on a cabinet or your tree—or set them on the serving platter,
    among other favorite cookies. Store the cookies in an airtight container at
    room temperature for up to 1 week.

How to Host a
SUGAR COOKIE DECORATING PARTY

Make your way to our sugar cookie soiree—bring your favorite Christmas cookie cutters, sprinkles, and sugar toppings for elftastic cookie creations!

BEFORE GUESTS ARRIVE

- Make Christmas Cheer Punch (page 74) and Meat Us at the Wreath (page 69) for snacking.
- Prepare one or two batches of dough (48 to 96 cookies) from Bright Light Sugar Cookies (page 60). Plan on each person making 6 cookies.

- Prepare 3 to 6 cups Mrs. Claus' Royal Icing (page 10). Reserve thicker icing for outlining the cookies. Separate portions of icing for tinting into smaller bowls or cups. Thin with 1 to 2 drops water, then tint by dropping a small amount of color off the tip of a toothpick. Stir. Add more until your desired color is achieved. Cover with plastic wrap until ready to use.

WHEN GUESTS ARRIVE

- Offer a big, warm welcome—a smile, a hug, or maybe even a Christmas song!

- Line sheet pans with parchment paper. Dust cutting boards or a clean work surface with flour, then give each person a small amount of cookie dough. Roll out the dough and cut out shapes. Place the cutouts on the prepared sheet pans and refrigerate until firm, 20 to 30 minutes—this helps keep the cookies from spreading when baking.

- Position two oven racks, evenly spaced, in the center of the oven. Preheat the oven to 350°F.

- Transfer the cookies from the refrigerator to the oven and bake in batches, switching the pans on the oven racks halfway through, until the cookies are lightly browned around the edges, 10 to 12 minutes. Cool on the pan on a wire rack for 10 minutes, then transfer the cookies directly to the rack to cool thoroughly before decorating.

- Time to decorate! Refer to Mrs. Claus' Sugar Cookie Decorating Tips (page 11). Let the icing set slightly, then decorate with sprinkles or sanding sugar.

- Eat, drink, and be merry!

Spread Christmas cheer by sharing a tray of your cookie creations with neighbors or a shelter, hospital, or retirement home.

It's cookie time!

Peanut Butter
PIKKU DEER COOKIES

**MAKES ABOUT
1½ DOZEN COOKIES**

These cookies look just like the tiny Pikku reindeer that live with us at the North Pole! (You can see them for yourself in the animated special *Elf Pets: Santa's Reindeer Rescue*.) Pikku reindeer, like your Elf Pets reindeer, can help the sleigh soar on Christmas Eve powered by your good cheer and special care.

FOR THE COOKIE DOUGH

- ☐ 2 cups all-purpose flour, plus more for dusting
- ☐ 2¾ teaspoons pumpkin pie spice
- ☐ 1 teaspoon baking powder
- ☐ ½ teaspoon kosher salt
- ☐ ½ cup (1 stick) unsalted butter, at room temperature
- ☐ ½ cup creamy peanut butter
- ☐ ½ cup granulated sugar
- ☐ ½ cup packed dark brown sugar
- ☐ 1 large egg
- ☐ 1 large egg yolk
- ☐ 1 teaspoon pure vanilla extract

SPECIAL EQUIPMENT

3-inch gingerbread person cookie cutter

Pastry bag fitted with small round tip

1. Make the dough: In a large bowl, whisk together the flour, pumpkin pie spice, baking powder, and salt. Set aside.
2. In the bowl of a stand mixer fitted with the paddle attachment (or another large bowl, if using a handheld mixer), beat the butter, peanut butter, granulated sugar, and brown sugar on medium-high speed until light and fluffy, 3 to 5 minutes. Add the egg, egg yolk, and vanilla, then mix on low speed to incorporate.
3. Add the flour mixture to the butter mixture and continue to mix on low speed, about 30 seconds. Stop and scrape down the sides of the bowl, then continue mixing until a dough forms, 30 seconds more.
4. Divide the dough evenly into 2 balls. Wrap each ball in plastic wrap and shape it into a flat disk about ½ inch thick. Refrigerate for 1 hour.
5. Line 2 sheet pans with parchment paper. Lightly flour a work surface. Working with 1 disk at a time, roll to ¼ inch thick. Cut out shapes and transfer them to the prepared sheet pans, arranging them 1 inch apart. Gather any dough scraps, pat them into a ball, reroll, and cut out more shapes. Refrigerate until firm, 20 to 30 minutes.
6. Position two oven racks, evenly spaced, in the center of the oven. Preheat the oven to 350°F.

STEP 1

STEP 2

STEP 3

FOR DECORATING

☐ 1 cup Mrs. Claus' Royal Icing (page 10) or store-bought cookie icing

☐ 18 brown candy-coated chocolates, for noses

☐ 36 candy eyeballs

☐ 9 to 10 pretzel thins, halved

7. Transfer the cookies from the refrigerator to the oven and bake, switching the pans on the oven racks halfway through, until the cookies are lightly browned around the edges, 8 to 10 minutes. Cool on the pan on a wire rack for 10 minutes, then transfer the cookies directly to the rack to cool completely before decorating.

8. To decorate: Refer to Mrs. Claus' Sugar Cookie Decorating Tips (page 11) if needed. Rotate the gingerbread cookie so the legs become antlers at the top of the reindeer's head. Fill the pastry bag with the icing and draw ears, eyes, and a mouth on the reindeer. Use the icing to attach the chocolate nose, candy eyeballs, and pretzel halves for antlers. So a-deerable! Store the cookies in an airtight container at room temperature for up to 1 week.

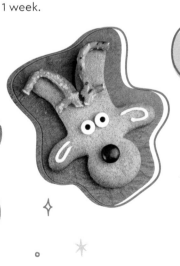

Let's name him S'norms!

DECK THE HALLS!

Salami Roses

Santa's favorite fruit is oranges! What's yours?

Scout Elves LOVE pomegranate seeds.

Meat Us at the WREATH

- 15 rosemary sprigs, 5 to 6 inches in length
- One 16-ounce pepperoni stick, cut into ½-inch slices (about 30 slices)
- 40 slices Genoa salami (from ½ pound), to make 4 Salami Roses (see Sweet Shop Secret)
- One 8-ounce bunch seedless red or green grapes, broken into smaller bunches
- 2 medium navel oranges, separated into segments
- 10 to 12 mixed dried fruit slices or rings, such as peach, orange, or apple
- One 8-ounce block cheese, such as Cheddar, Colby, or Monterey Jack, cut lengthwise into two 1-inch-thick sheets
- ½ cup Mexican Hot Chocolate Candied Nuts (page 164) or mixed nuts
- ½ cup pomegranate seeds
- 1 box mini festive-shape crackers or cookies, such as Christmas tree crackers, gingerbread people, or holiday shortbreads
- Sage and/or thyme sprigs and bay leaves

SPECIAL EQUIPMENT

Large charcuterie board or round serving platter, about 15 inches in diameter

1½-inch star-shaped (or other fun small-shaped) vegetable or cookie cutters

Festive ribbon

Even Scout Elves need a break from cookies and confections. So, we're glad you saw us here with caref'lly planned directions. We've circled round to figure out the dish we thought would please And landed on a wreath composed of savory meat and cheese!

1. Prepare the base: Arrange the rosemary sprigs on the charcuterie board in a circular shape to form the wreath. The greenery will serve as your border.
2. Arrange the meats: Arrange the pepperoni and salami roses around the inside of the wreath, allowing space in between for other ingredients.
3. Arrange the fruit: Arrange the grapes bunches, orange segments, and mixed dried fruit between the meats, allowing space for the remaining ingredients.
4. Cut and arrange the cheese, nuts, and seeds: Use the vegetable or cookie cutters to make decorative cheese cubes and arrange them to fill in the empty spaces. Scatter the nuts and pomegranate seeds around the wreath for crunch and color.
5. Final touches: Fill in any remaining gaps with savory crackers or sweet cookies, followed by sprigs of herbs and festive ribbon.

SWEET SHOP SECRET

Salami Roses

Fold a piece of salami over the rim of a glass with a narrow mouth, such as a small juice glass. Repeat the process with 8 to 10 more slices salami, overlapping the slices as you work your way around the glass. Invert the glass onto a clean surface, slide the salami out, and ho ho hooray! Salami as "rosy" as Santa's cheeks.

Cookie Star STACKS

MAKES ABOUT 20 LARGE STAR COOKIES AND 20 ELF-SIZE STAR COOKIES

FOR THE COOKIE DOUGH

- 2 cups all-purpose flour, plus more for dusting
- ½ cup unsweetened cocoa powder
- ½ teaspoon baking powder
- ¼ teaspoon kosher salt
- ½ pound (2 sticks) unsalted butter, at room temperature
- 1 cup granulated sugar
- 1 large egg
- 1 teaspoon peppermint extract

FOR DECORATING

- Festive mini candy-coated chocolates or other small candy
- Powdered sugar

SPECIAL EQUIPMENT

2½-inch star-shaped cookie cutters

1½-inch star-shaped cookie cutters

When the bright beams of the North Star shine down on the North Pole, Santa gathers us to share the State of the World's Christmas Spirit. In honor of that momentous occasion, we give you this recipe to make North Star–shaped cookies. The faith, hope, and love you put into making them will be used to make Christmas magic!

1. In a large bowl, whisk together the flour, cocoa powder, baking powder, and salt.
2. In the bowl of a stand mixer fitted with the paddle attachment (or another large bowl, if using a handheld mixer), beat together the butter and granulated sugar on medium speed until pale and fluffy, 3 to 5 minutes. Add the egg and peppermint extract, then mix on low speed until incorporated.
3. Add the flour mixture to the butter mixture and continue to mix on low speed, about 30 seconds. Stop and scrape down the sides of the bowl, then continue mixing until a dough forms, about 30 seconds more.
4. Divide the dough evenly into 2 balls. Wrap each ball in plastic wrap and shape it into a flat disk about ½ inch thick. Refrigerate for 1 hour.

(recipe continues on page 72)

THE ELF ON THE SHELF FAMILY COOKBOOK

5. Line 2 sheet pans with parchment paper. Lightly flour a work surface. Working with 1 disk at a time, roll it out to ¼ inch thick. Using the 2½-inch star cutter, cut out shapes. Transfer them to the prepared sheet pans, arranging them about 1 inch apart. Using the 1½-inch star cutter, cut out the center of each cookie. Arrange the small star cutouts in the empty spaces. Gather the dough scraps, pat them into a ball, reroll, and cut out more shapes. Refrigerate until firm, 20 to 30 minutes.

6. Position two oven racks, evenly spaced, in the center of the oven. Preheat the oven to 350°F.

7. Bake, switching the pans on the racks halfway through, until your kitchen smells like a candy cane and the cookies are firm to the touch, 8 to 10 minutes. Cool the cookies on the pan on a wire rack for 10 minutes, then transfer them directly to the rack to cool completely.

8. Your Scout Elves may stack the cookies and place small candies inside. They'll top them with a small star "lid" and dust with powdered sugar. Store the cookies in an airtight container at room temperature for up to 1 week.

North Pole Fact: Red and green candies hold extra Christmas cheer! Star light, star bright, how many candies feel just right?

It looks like Christmas magic to me!

CHRISTMAS *Cheer* PUNCH

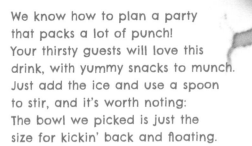

MAKES 8 SERVINGS

We know how to plan a party
that packs a lot of punch!
Your thirsty guests will love this
drink, with yummy snacks to munch.
Just add the ice and use a spoon
to stir, and it's worth noting:
The bowl we picked is just the
size for kickin' back and floating.

- ☐ 3 cups fresh or frozen cranberries
- ☐ 1 large navel orange, sliced into half-moons
- ☐ 1 lime, thinly sliced
- ☐ 8 cups (2 quarts) chilled cranberry or pomegranate juice
- ☐ 4 cups (1 quart) chilled apple cider
- ☐ 2 cups chilled ginger ale (for a less sweet punch, use sparkling water instead)

1. Scatter the cranberries, orange, and lime in the Bundt pan. Fill with ½ cup of the cranberry juice and enough water to submerge the fruit by 1 inch. Freeze until solid, at least 2 hours.
2. Invert the Bundt pan under warm water until the fruit ring easily slips out, then transfer the frozen ring to the punch bowl—this keeps your punch cold!
3. Pour the remaining 7½ cups juice, the apple cider, and ginger ale over the ring. Use a wooden spoon to gently stir, then serve!

SPECIAL EQUIPMENT

Standard 10- to 12-cup Bundt pan

1-gallon punch bowl

Party Punch FOR GROWN-UPS

RUM PUNCH: Stir in 1 cup spiced rum for a jolly good warm and toasty punch full of vanilla and clove flavors.

VODKA PUNCH: Stir in 1 cup plain or flavored vodka, such as hot cinnamon, orange, or vanilla, for a spirited punch.

WINE PUNCH: Stir in one 750 ml bottle dry red wine, such as Cabernet Sauvignon, for a heartwarming velvety-rich punch.

A PARTY in a Pan TREAT

MAKES ABOUT 2 DOZEN TREATS

On the twelfth day of Christmas, your Scout Elves gave to you . . . 12 gooey chocolate chip cookies, 11 mini pretzels, 10 petite candy bars, 9 ounces baking chips, 8 tiny candy canes, 70 mini marshmallows, 6 ounces salted mixed nuts, 5 tablespoons Golden Cheer, 14 ounces sweetened condensed milk, 3 tablespoons festive sprinkles, and ²/₃ cup coconut . . . to make A Party in a Pan Treat!

- ☐ One 16-ounce package ready-to-bake cookie dough, such as chocolate chip or sugar, divided into 12 equal (1¼-ounce) portions
- ☐ 11 mini pretzels, crushed
- ☐ 10 mini candy bars (any kind), chopped (4 ounces total)
- ☐ 9 ounces baking chips, any flavor, such as peanut butter or butterscotch
- ☐ 8 mini candy canes, crushed
- ☐ 70 mini marshmallows
- ☐ 6 ounces salted mixed nuts
- ☐ 5 tablespoons Golden Cheer (page 25)
- ☐ One 14-ounce can sweetened condensed milk
- ☐ 3 heaping tablespoons festive sprinkles
- ☐ ²/₃ cup unsweetened finely shredded coconut
- ☐ Sea salt (optional)

SPECIAL EQUIPMENT
9 × 13-inch baking pan

1. Preheat the oven to 350°F. Line the baking pan with parchment paper, allowing a 2-inch overhang on all sides.
2. Equally space the cookie dough portions in the prepared baking pan. Gently press to create an even layer. Bake until the cookies spread and form a soft, uniform crust, about 10 minutes.
3. In a large bowl, combine the pretzels, candy bars, baking chips, candy canes, marshmallows, nuts, and Golden Cheer. Add the condensed milk and stir until a sticky, thick mixture forms. Spread the mixture over the par-baked cookie crust, forming a compact layer. Combine the sprinkles and coconut in a small bowl, then scatter evenly across the top of the candy-nut mixture.
4. Bake until the coconut is browned at the edges, 30 minutes. Transfer the pan to a wire rack to cool completely for 1 hour. When cool, chill in the refrigerator for 30 minutes.
5. Using the parchment paper overhang, lift the treat out of the pan and place on a cutting board. Using a sharp knife, cut into about twenty-four 2-inch-square treats. Sprinkle with sea salt if you wish.

CAROL CONUNDRUM

Our favorite classic Christmas carols and North Pole songs have been swapped for wacky alternates! We're scratching our caps as we try to figure out which is which! Can you?

"C'mon Freezing, Fluffy White Stuff!"

"Jangly Ring-a-Lings"

"Hoppyhappyhootenannyous"

"Elves on the Endless Energy Express"

"Flurry Feet"

"O Holiday Houseplant"

"I Closed My Eyes and Hoped a Big Thought for Your Joyful Christmas Days"

"Pooches Peering Through Shiny Glass"

"Yuletide Yippees Around the Corner"

"Eleven Plus One Day of Wacky Presents"

"Wreath Wrangling in the Hallway"

"Our Boss Is on the Way to Where You Live"

→ See music videos for some of these songs on The Elf on the Shelf channel on YouTube!

THE ELF ON THE SHELF FAMILY COOKBOOK

SONG BANK

"Deck the Halls"

"Wishing You a Little Merry Joyful Upbeat Happy Jubilant Christmas Day"

"Jingle Bells"

"Extravaganzalorious"

"Scout Elves Don't Rest"

"Snowflake Shuffle"

"O Christmas Tree"

"Pups at the Window"

"Christmas Cheer Is Near"

"The Twelve Days of Christmas"

"Santa Claus Is Coming to Town"

"Let It Snow!"

Psst . . . Over here. Do you know what special talent Santa has besides being wise, kind, and our Jolliest Boss? That's right! He plays the drums!

Christmas Carol KARAOKE

Singing Christmas carols drums up Christmas cheer! Play this fun Christmas karaoke game and serve A Party in a Pan Treat (page 77) after the performances.

BEFORE YOU BEGIN

1. Prepare a list of favorite Christmas carols or North Pole songs.
2. Print the lyrics.
3. Find the instrumental version of the song to play, or be prepared to hum the tune for the participant to sing to.
4. Write the name of each song on a slip of paper and place it in a Santa hat.

HOW TO PLAY

1. Draw the name of a song from the hat.
2. Set a timer for 3 minutes to memorize the verses.
3. Play the tune and sing the carol. Bonus for using props!
4. The participant with the most applause wins!

Decked Out DIPPERS

Join us as we deck out treats and snacks with silky-smooth chocolate and sprinkles. Eat them up or use them as North Polar props in The Sweetest Shop (page 148). Check out the ideas on the following pages, choose your favorites, then dip and repeat, treat after treat!

FOR DIPPING

- ☐ Two to four 12-ounce bags candy melts, assorted colors, depending on how many creations you wish to make!
- ☐ Apples, any color
- ☐ Biscotti, any flavor
- ☐ Conical corn snacks, such as Bugles
- ☐ Candy canes
- ☐ Graham cracker pieces and crumbs
- ☐ Mini marshmallows
- ☐ Pretzel rods
- ☐ Square shortbread cookies
- ☐ Sugar cones (#310 size), such as Joy brand

Dipping IDEAS

S'MORNAMENTS-ORNAMENTS: Scrub and thoroughly dry apples. Insert a skewer into the stem. Dip the entire apple in chocolate candy melt. Cover with graham cracker crumbs and mini marshmallows. To make colorful ornaments: Dip the entire apple in your choice of colored candy melt, then dip halfway in sanding sugar or sprinkles.

BISKITTI: Dip the ends of biscotti in white candy melt and cover with snowflake sprinkles.

ELF-SIZE CHRISTMAS TREES: Dip corn-shaped snacks, like Bugles, in green candy melt. Invert and decorate with sprinkles and stars.

SLED: Lay a graham cracker on a parchment-lined pan. Apply a generous amount of white candy melt along the long sides of the cracker. Attach 1 candy cane to each side, with the curved part hanging off the edges and the straight part running alongside the cracker. Lift the cracker and hold the candy canes in place until hardened, about 5 minutes (have patience!).

SANTA'S REINDEER: Dip pretzel rods two-thirds of the way in chocolate candy melt. Decorate with candy eyeballs and chocolate candy noses. Break a mini pretzel in half and attach to the sides for antlers.

CHRISTMAS GIFTS: Dip three square shortbread cookies all the way in your choice of colored candy melts. Let them dry slightly, then stack and decorate with sprinkles. Tie licorice laces around them for a bow, trimming them as needed.

SNOWFLAKES: Dip snowflake-shaped pretzels all the way in white candy melt. Cover with snowflake sprinkles.

PINE TREE FOREST: Dip a sugar cone in green candy melt. Invert and leave plain, to create a North Pole–inspired grove of trees, or decorate with sprinkles, stars, and candies for a Christmas tree. Or dip in white candy melt, let dry, and dust with colored luster dust for a shimmery tree. Refer to How to Use Luster Dust (page 7).

DECORATIONS

- ☐ Snowflakes, stars, and other festive sprinkles
- ☐ Assorted candies, including candy eyeballs, candy-coated chocolates, and licorice laces
- ☐ Sanding sugar, assorted colors
- ☐ Luster dust, assorted colors

SPECIAL EQUIPMENT
Decorative skewers

Dipping DIRECTIONS

1. Line several sheet pans with parchment paper. Fill small bowls with sanding sugars, if using. Place the melts in separate small microwave-safe bowls, dividing by color. Microwave the melts, uncovered, on high, in 30-second increments, stirring in between, until melted and smooth. Transfer the melts to tall glasses for easier dipping (for dipping apples, leave the melt in a bowl).
2. Working over the prepared sheet pans (for easy cleanup!), use a spoon or tongs to gently dip ingredients in the melts. Gently swirl or tap to remove excess.
3. Place each dipped item on a prepared sheet pan. Allow the candy melt to set for a few seconds before decorating or constructing, as directed.
4. Let your creation harden at room temperature, about 15 minutes. Gift, display, or keep an eye out for what your Scout Elves may do with them!

(Tiny) Trees for SALE!

Of all our jobs (and we've got lots!), this one makes us happy.
(Though sitting long with "Trees for Sale" does risk us getting sappy.)
We love to see your face light up when you see our elf-size trees.
Here are no-bake breezy steps to making more of these!

- ☐ Two 8-ounce boxes The Elf on the Shelf cake bites or other boxed individually wrapped mini holiday cakes
- ☐ 8 ounces dark green candy melts

FOR DECORATING
- ☐ 10 to 12 gold star-shaped sprinkles
- ☐ Sanding sugar, assorted colors

SPECIAL EQUIPMENT
Toothpick

1. Line a sheet pan with parchment paper and set aside.
2. In a large bowl, use a wooden spoon to mash the cake bites until they have the consistency of Play-Doh. Using your clean hands, shape various-size cake balls and place them on the prepared sheet pan. Form each ball into a cone-shaped tree with a flat bottom. Chill the trees in the freezer before dipping, about 15 minutes.
3. Place the melts in a small microwave-safe bowl. Microwave on high, uncovered, in 30-second increments, stirring in between, until melted and smooth. Working with 1 tree at a time, drop it in the candy melt. Use a spoon to gently coat, then roll the tree onto a fork to lift it out. Gently tap the fork handle against the rim of the bowl—this will remove any excess. Roll the tree off the fork and stand it upright on the prepared sheet pan. Repeat with the remaining trees. Let the candy melt set, about 10 minutes.

4. Reheat the remaining candy melt, if necessary, by returning it to the microwave. When the trees are set, use the toothpick to add a thick row of melt encircling the bottom of the tree. While still wet, sprinkle with sanding sugar to create tinsel. Allow the trees to dry completely. Add two more tinsel rows going up the tree, drying between each row.

5. Arrange your magical forest of trees on a serving platter or on the counter—they're "for sale!" Store in an airtight container at room temperature for 2 days or in the refrigerator for up to 1 week.

Legends and Lore
SCROLL COOKIES

Scout Elf Joe, whose North Pole knowledge is second only to Santa's, takes great pride in working at the North Pole Legends and Lore Laboratory. While Elf Joe works with top-secret North Pole information stored in books and scrolls, we got ahold of his recipe for making these golden scroll cookies filled with cinnamon and sugar. He's so into his job that he sleeps, dreams, and eats it!

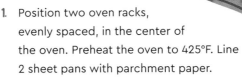

- ☐ 2 tablespoons granulated sugar
- ☐ 2 teaspoons ground cinnamon
- ☐ 4 tablespoons yellow sanding sugar
- ☐ 2 sheets frozen puff pastry sheets (from one 17-ounce package), thawed

1. Position two oven racks, evenly spaced, in the center of the oven. Preheat the oven to 425°F. Line 2 sheet pans with parchment paper.

2. In a small bowl, stir together the granulated sugar and cinnamon.

3. Sprinkle 1 tablespoon of the sanding sugar on one of the prepared sheet pans. Unroll 1 sheet of the puff pastry over the sugar. Scatter 1 tablespoon of the sanding sugar evenly over the top of the pastry sheet. Using a rolling pin, roll over the pastry sheet to adhere the sugar on both sides. Scatter half of the cinnamon sugar mixture over the top of the pastry sheet.

4. Using your fingers, tightly roll the long side of the pastry into the center, like a scroll. Roll the opposite side into the center to meet it. Cut the scroll crosswise into ½-inch-thick pieces; you should have about 10 scroll cookie pieces. Arrange the cookie pieces on their sides about 1 inch apart on the prepared sheet pan.

5. Repeat the process on the second prepared sheet pan with the remaining pastry sheet, using the remaining 2 tablespoons sanding sugar and remaining cinnamon-sugar mixture.

6. Bake until the tops are golden and the bottoms are crisp, about 5 minutes. Flip the cookies, switch the pans on the oven racks, and continue baking until golden on the other side, 5 minutes more.

7. Cool on a wire rack for 10 minutes, then transfer the cookies directly to the rack to cool completely. Store the cookies in an airtight container at room temperature for up to 1 week.

$E = mc^2$

Santa's sleigh has a reserved parking spot in North Pole City Center.

RESERVED PARKING

THE BIG GUY

Santa needs **YOUR** Christmas cheer to make Christmas magic—without it, the sleigh wouldn't lift off the ground!

Santa's "Ho ho ho!" can be heard up to **100** miles away.

Before we can be adopted by families as Reporting Scout Elves, we must graduate from Scout Elf School.

north Pole FUN FACTS

H_2O

start

We compete in the **North Pole Candy Cane Challenge** each September— a timed obstacle course. The fastest Scout Elf wins!

Scout Elves can throw **4sps,** or "snowballs per second."

Record

The all-time record for the SESSC—Scout Elf Sitting Still Contest—is sixteen days without moving or blinking!

FiNiSH

Since we cannot fly before we are adopted and named, we train in a wind tunnel. **wheeee!**

MAKES AS MANY AS YOU LIKE!

Last night, this fresh take on an old song gave us a great idea: "Deck the halls with lots of lollies. Fa-la-la-la-la-la lollipops!" Thread fresh fruit on lollipop sticks any way you wish, then dip in marshmallow cream and lick! Check out the ideas below, then choose a lolly to make and decorate. Whatever you choose, it's sure to be a jolly good lolly!

FOR THE LOLLIPOPS

- ☐ Lemon juice, for dipping
- ☐ Bananas, cut into thirds, thick coins, or cutouts
- ☐ Blackberries
- ☐ Blueberries
- ☐ Cantaloupe cubes and cutouts
- ☐ Green grapes
- ☐ Honeydew cubes and cutouts
- ☐ Kiwi
- ☐ Clementine or navel orange segments
- ☐ Pineapple cubes and cutouts
- ☐ Raspberries
- ☐ Shredded coconut
- ☐ Star fruit (also called carambola), edges trimmed, cut crosswise
- ☐ Hulled strawberries, whole and slices
- ☐ Watermelon cubes and cutouts

Fa-la-la IDEAS

SNOWPERSON: Thread 3 banana coins, flat side facing out, for the snowperson's body. Top with a mini peppermint patty for the hat brim, 1 whole strawberry for the hat, and a mini marshmallow hat topper. Decorate with sugar pearls for eyes, and buttons and orange sprinkles for the nose.

SANTA: Dip ⅓ medium banana in lemon juice. Roll it in coconut to make Santa's beard, then thread. Top with ⅓ standard marshmallow for the hat brim, 1 whole strawberry for the hat, and a mini marshmallow hat topper. Decorate with black sugar pearls for the eyes and nose.

TINY TINSEL: Alternate threading colorful fruits, such as grapes, berries, clementines, and star fruit. Paint the fruit with luster dust for a shiny tinsel effect. Refer to How to Use Luster Dust (page 7).

CANDY CANE: Alternate threading banana coins with peppermint patties and strawberry slices.

TREE TOPPERS: Alternate threading your choice of fruit, such as blueberries, raspberries, and pineapple, then top with star fruit slices or fruit cutouts, such as a star, snowperson, tree, or ornament. Dip the top of the lollipop in lemon juice, followed by coconut for a "snowy" effect.

FOR DECORATING

☐ Standard marshmallows, sliced crosswise into thirds

☐ Mini marshmallows, assorted colors

☐ Mini peppermint patties

☐ Black and other color sugar pearls

☐ Gold and silver luster dust

☐ Festive sprinkles

SPECIAL EQUIPMENT

1½-inch star-shaped vegetable or cookie cutters, or other mini festive shapes (optional)

6-inch cake-pop sticks

Food-safe decorating brushes

Threading DIRECTIONS

1. Line several sheet pans with parchment paper. Fill a small bowl with lemon juice. Place the cut-up fruit in separate bowls, dividing by type or color.

2. Thread fruit cubes, slices, and cutouts onto the cake-pop sticks, as desired.

3. Decorate the sticks and arrange them on the prepared sheet pan. Serve immediately with dip.

Marshmallow CREAM DIP

1. In a medium bowl, whisk the yogurt and marshmallow cream until smooth and creamy. Add the vanilla and mix until well incorporated.

2. Transfer the dip to a small serving bowl. Top with sprinkles just before serving.

MAKES ABOUT 1 CUP

☐ ½ cup plain Greek or vanilla yogurt

☐ ½ cup marshmallow cream

☐ ½ teaspoon pure vanilla extract

☐ Festive sprinkles, for garnish

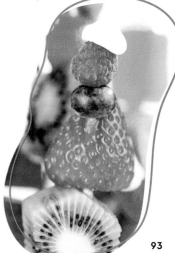

Elfprint COOKIES

FOR THE COOKIE DOUGH

- 1½ cups all-purpose flour, plus more for dusting
- ¼ teaspoon kosher salt
- 11 tablespoons (1⅓ sticks) unsalted butter, at room temperature
- ½ cup granulated sugar
- 2 large egg yolks
- 1 teaspoon pure vanilla extract
- ½ cup sanding sugar, any color
- About 1 cup jam or preserves, such as raspberry

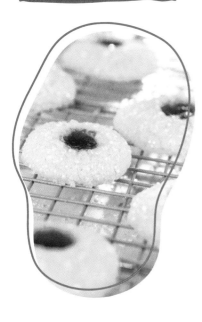

We thought we'd bake a cookie treat—'twas not our finest plan. Our project turned catastrophous—there are elfprints in the jam!

1. In a medium bowl, whisk together the flour and salt.
2. In the bowl of a stand mixer fitted with the paddle attachment (or a large bowl, if using a handheld mixer), beat together the butter and sugar on medium-high speed until pale and fluffy, about 3 minutes. Add the egg yolks and vanilla, then mix on low speed to incorporate.
3. Add the flour mixture to the butter mixture and continue to mix on low speed, about 30 seconds. Stop and scrape down the sides of the bowl, then continue mixing until a dough forms, about 30 seconds more.
4. Wrap the dough ball in plastic wrap and shape it into a flat disk about ½ inch thick. Refrigerate for 1 hour.
5. Line 2 sheet pans with parchment paper. Place the sanding sugar in a small bowl.
6. Using your clean hands, pull off pieces of dough and roll them into balls the size of a grape (¼ ounce each), then roll in the sanding sugar to coat. Place the balls about 1 inch apart on the prepared sheet pans. Using your pinky, gently make an elf-size footprint in the center of each dough ball. If the edges crack, use your fingers to smooth them. Refrigerate until firm, 20 to 30 minutes.
7. Position two oven racks, evenly spaced, in the center of the oven. Preheat the oven to 350°F.
8. Fill each cookie indentation with ½ teaspoon jam. Bake, switching the pans on the racks halfway through, until the bottoms are lightly browned, about 10 minutes.
9. Cool on the pans on a wire rack for 10 minutes, then transfer the cookies directly to the rack to cool completely. Store the cookies in an airtight container at room temperature for up to 1 week.

Candy Cane Crash CUPCAKES

MAKES 1 DOZEN CUPCAKES AND 2½ DOZEN CAKE BALL ORNAMENTS

After you all hit the hay, we had the house to ourselves for baking, dancing to carols on the radio, and swinging on the chandeliers with our candy cane cables . . .

And that's when it happened . . . **CRASH**!!!!!!!!
(We're okay, just a teensy tinsel tumble.)

But we sincerely apologize for the broken baubles and crumbled canes caused by our collision.

FOR THE CUPCAKES

- ☐ Cooking spray
- ☐ 2½ cups all-purpose flour
- ☐ 2½ teaspoons baking powder
- ☐ 1 teaspoon kosher salt
- ☐ 2 cups sugar
- ☐ 4 large eggs
- ☐ 1 cup vegetable oil
- ☐ 1 teaspoon peppermint extract
- ☐ ⅔ cup whole milk
- ☐ 4 cups peppermint buttercream (see page 9)

1. Preheat the oven to 350°F. Grease the muffin tin cups with cooking spray, and line the cups of one of the tins with paper liners (one tin of cupcakes will be used to create the cake ball ornaments, so no need to line it). Line a sheet pan with parchment paper.
2. Make the cupcake batter: In a medium bowl, whisk together the flour, baking powder, and salt.
3. In the bowl of a stand mixer fitted with the whisk attachment (or a large bowl, if using a handheld mixer), beat together the sugar and eggs on medium-high speed until pale and fluffy, about 2 minutes. Add the vegetable oil and peppermint extract, then mix on low speed to incorporate. Add the flour mixture in three additions, alternating with the milk. Stop and scrape down the side of the bowl as needed. Divide the batter evenly among the muffin tins, filling each cup two-thirds full.

(recipe continues on next page)

DECK THE HALLS!

97

FOR THE ORNAMENTS

- ☐ Two 12-ounce bags red candy melts
- ☐ About 30 mini white or milk chocolate peanut butter cups
- ☐ ½ teaspoon gold luster dust
- ☐ Festive sprinkles, any color

SPECIAL EQUIPMENT

Two 12-cup muffin tins

12 cupcake liners

Toothpick

Food-safe decorating brush

Pastry bag fitted with an open star tip

4. Bake until the tops of the cupcakes are golden brown and the toothpick inserted in the center of one comes out clean, 20 to 25 minutes. Cool on the pan on a wire rack for 10 minutes, then transfer the cupcakes directly to the rack to cool completely.

5. Make the cake ball ornaments: Place the 12 unlined cupcakes in the bowl of a food processor and pulse until finely crumbed. Transfer to a large bowl, add 1½ cups of the frosting, and stir until the mixture is smooth and doughy. Refrigerate for 30 minutes.

6. Using your clean hands, shape the cake dough into about 30 gumball-size cake balls (about 1 ounce each). Place them on the prepared sheet pan. Chill in the freezer for 15 minutes.

7. Meanwhile, place the candy melts in a microwave-safe bowl. Microwave on high, uncovered, in 30-second increments, stirring in between, until melted and smooth.

8. Working with 1 ball at a time, roll it with your hands one more time until very smooth, then drop it in the candy melt. Use a spoon to gently coat it, then roll the ball onto a fork to lift it out. Gently tap the fork handle against the rim of the bowl—this will remove any excess chocolate. Roll the ball off the fork onto the prepared sheet pan. Repeat with the remaining balls.

THE ELF ON THE SHELF FAMILY COOKBOOK

9. Apply a spot of candy melt to the top of a peanut butter cup, invert, and attach to a cake ball to make the ornament cap. Allow the candy melt to harden, about 10 minutes. Using the brush, dust the cake ball and ornament cap with luster dust to add shine! Repeat with the remaining balls.

10. Fill and decorate the cupcakes: Using a knife, cut a hole in the center of each cupcake, about 1 inch across and 1 inch deep. Fill the holes with sprinkles. (Eat the cupcake cutout!) Fill the pastry bag halfway with buttercream. Holding the bag at a 90-degree angle, start at the outer edge of the cupcake and squeeze the bag, piping a circle, and working inward, two times. Pull upward to finish. Use a knife to slice ("break") 12 cake ball ornaments in half and place both halves in the center of each cupcake. Arrange the remaining unbroken ornaments alongside. Bite into a cupcake crash—spill, jolly folly!

CHAPTER 3

MERRY MOVIE NIGHT MELTS & MUNCHIES

STARRING:
YOUR SCOUT ELVES

DIRECTED BY:
SANTA CLAUS

★★★★★
"FiVE stars!"

"Merry Movie Night with my Elf Pets was epic!! The snuggles were so satisfying–just like the melty munchies my mom and dad made for us!"
–Amani, seven, from Chicago

Melty, Munchie
MOVIE NIGHT BOARD

We like our movie snacks to be like our holiday movies—lots of colors, heart melting, and full of Christmas joy. Here's an elftastic idea for you: make this melty munchie board worthy of being the star of the show.

1. Make the star sandwiches: Lay the bread slices on a clean work surface and cut out shapes with the cookie cutter. You should get two shapes from each slice, to make 8 star sandwiches total. (Snack on the bread edges.)

2. Spread 1 tablespoon of cream cheese evenly on one side of 8 bread stars, followed by 2 to 3 strawberry slices. Top with the remaining 8 bread stars.

(recipe continues on next page)

FOR STRAWBERRY STAR SANDWICHES
MAKES 8 SANDWICHES
- 8 slices soft, thick whole wheat or white sandwich bread (look for one labeled "country style" or "farmhouse")
- ½ cup strawberry cream cheese, at room temperature
- 6 to 8 strawberries, stems removed, sliced

FOR MELTED HAM, JAM, AND CHEESE TOASTIES
MAKES 8 TOASTIES
- 16 frozen mini waffles, toasted
- About ¼ cup fruit preserves, such as peach, apricot, or orange
- 4 slices deli ham, cut in half
- 4 slices deli American, Cheddar, or Swiss cheese, cut in half
- 2 tablespoons unsalted butter, plus more as needed

SPECIAL EQUIPMENT
2½-inch Christmas star or other Christmas shape cookie cutter

Large serving platter or cutting board

FOR PEPPERONI PINWHEELS

MAKES 16 PINWHEELS

- ☐ 2 spinach wraps or burrito-size tortillas, 10 to 12 inches in diameter
- ☐ ½ cup vegetable cream cheese
- ☐ 20 slices deli pepperoni, thinly sliced
- ☐ 10 slices deli salami, thinly sliced
- ☐ 8 slices American, Cheddar, or Swiss cheese
- ☐ 1 cup packed baby spinach leaves

FOR SERVING

- ☐ Cherry tomatoes (optional)
- ☐ Reindeer Munch Snack Mix (page 113)
- ☐ Jolly Holly Popcorn Balls (page 118)
- ☐ Potato chips
- ☐ Festive pretzels, plain, or decked out (see page 82)
- ☐ Celery sticks
- ☐ Carrot sticks

3. Make the toasties: On a clean work surface, lay out 8 of the waffles. Spread about 1 teaspoon of fruit preserves evenly on one side of each waffle. Top each waffle with a ½ slice of ham, followed by a ½ slice of cheese, folding, trimming, or tucking the ham and cheese into the waffle so they don't hang out too much! Top with the remaining 8 waffles.

4. In a large nonstick skillet over medium heat, melt the butter. Working in batches, and melting more butter if necessary, add the toasties and cook until the cheese is melted, about 3 minutes, flipping once during cooking.

5. Make the pinwheels: Lay the wraps on a clean work surface. Divide the cream cheese evenly between the 2 wraps and spread to completely cover. Cover each wrap with 10 pepperoni slices, 5 salami slices, and 4 cheese slices. Distribute the spinach leaves evenly on top. Roll the wraps closed, tucking as you go, then place them seam side down on the work surface. Using a serrated knife, cut each wrap into 8 even pinwheels.

6. Assemble the board: Arrange or stack the stars, toasties, and pinwheels around the platter, using the photo on page 102 as a guide. Fill in the spaces with small bowls of cherry tomatoes, Reindeer Munch, Jolly Holly Popcorn Balls, potato chips, pretzels, and/or celery and carrot sticks. Movie, munch, repeat!

THE ELF ON THE SHELF FAMILY COOKBOOK

merry Movie Night
SCAVENGER HUNT

Play this scavenger hunt game while viewing *Elf Pets: A Fox Cub's Christmas Tale*, *Elf Pets: Santa's Saint Bernard Saves Christmas*, *Elf Pets: Santa's Reindeer Rescue*, or *An Elf's Story*. The items below appear in each movie—keep an eye out for each one! Snuggle with your Elf Pets under a blanket fort with a Mug'nificent Cocoa (page 42).

Snowperson

Newsey Noel's camera

Letter for Santa

Hot cocoa

Cello

Handbell

Gym Dandy's whistle

Chippey's stocking

Christmas North Star

Snow globe pendant

Pikku deer

Barry

scout Elf COCOA BOMBS

For movie night (or any time!),
we have the perfect choice.
These yummy melty cocoa bombs
will make you all rejoice!
Just plop them in a mug and pour
hot milk right o'er the top,
or if you want to make a splash,
be careful when it drops!

- ¼ teaspoon red luster dust
- 6 ounces red candy melts
- 9 tablespoons Mrs. Claus' Santa-Size Batch of Cocoa Mix (page 40) or store-bought mix
- 24 mini marshmallows
- ½ cup semisweet chocolate chips
- 2 ounces white candy melts

TO SERVE

- ¾ cup (6 ounces) whole milk per serving, heated

SPECIAL EQUIPMENT

Pastry brush

Two (2.5-inch-diameter) silicone chocolate molds, with 6 molds each

Toothpick

12 Christmas-themed mini cupcake liners (optional)

1. Line a sheet pan with parchment paper. Using the pastry brush, dust the inside cups of the molds, including the edges, with the luster dust.
2. Place the red candy melts in a medium microwave-safe bowl. Microwave on high, uncovered, in 30-second increments, stirring in between, until melted and smooth. Spoon 1 teaspoon of the melt into the cup of each mold. Using the back of the spoon, spread to completely cover the cup, making sure to pull upward to coat the edges. Place the molds in the refrigerator to set, about 5 minutes.
3. If after 5 minutes the edges of the mold seem thin, apply a second, thin layer of the melt as needed. Return to the refrigerator to set, 3 minutes more. When set, gently unmold the shells and place them on the prepared sheet pan.
4. Warm a small skillet over medium heat, about 1 minute. Remove from the heat. Working with 1 shell at a time, gently melt the underside edges by touching it to the skillet for 2 seconds. Invert the shell and place it on the sheet pan. Fill with 1½ tablespoons cocoa mix, 4 marshmallows, and an elf-size portion of chocolate chips. Melt the edges of a second shell and attach the two halves by pressing the edges of the two shells together to create a round "bomb." Repeat with the remaining shells.

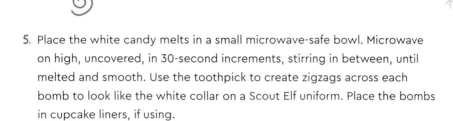

5. Place the white candy melts in a small microwave-safe bowl. Microwave on high, uncovered, in 30-second increments, stirring in between, until melted and smooth. Use the toothpick to create zigzags across each bomb to look like the white collar on a Scout Elf uniform. Place the bombs in cupcake liners, if using.

6. To make a cocoa bomb treat, place the bomb in a mug and pour hot milk over the top. Stir and watch the marshmallows float to the surface! Yum!

Mrs. Claus' North Pole Famous
PEPPERMINT BARK

MAKES 1 POUND

- ☐ 8 ounces bittersweet chocolate baking bar, finely chopped
- ☐ 1 teaspoon peppermint extract
- ☐ 8 ounces white chocolate baking bar, finely chopped
- ☐ 1 tablespoon coconut oil
- ☐ 6 regular or 12 mini candy canes, crushed (about ½ cup)

To all adorers of confection,

Announcing a sweet so divine, you'll be on cloud nine! Behold the peppermint bark. Our recipe, created by Mrs. Claus herself, is full of sweet minty pep to last you all season long!

Love,
YOUR SCOUT ELVES

1. Line a sheet pan with parchment paper and set aside.
2. Fill a medium saucepan with 2 inches of water and bring to a boil over high heat. Lower the heat to a simmer. Set a large heatproof bowl over the pan, making sure the bottom doesn't touch the water—it should hover above it. Add the bittersweet chocolate, stirring with a silicone spatula until melted. Stir in the peppermint extract, then remove the bowl from the heat.
3. Use the spatula to transfer the melted chocolate onto the prepared sheet pan. Spread the chocolate evenly, creating a thin, 11 × 7-inch rectangular layer, leaving about a 1½-inch border on all sides. Set aside. Clean the bowl.
4. Combine the white chocolate and coconut oil in the clean bowl. Add more water to the saucepan, if necessary, and return to a simmer. Repeat the process, stirring often, until the white chocolate is melted. Pour the white chocolate over the bittersweet chocolate layer and use the spatula to swirl the chocolates together. Scatter the crushed candy canes evenly on top. Refrigerate, uncovered, until firm, about 1 hour.
5. Use the tip of a sharp knife to break the bark into bite-size pieces before serving. Store the bark in an airtight container at room temperature for up to 3 days or in the refrigerator for up to 1 week.

Loading Christmas Spirit...

THE ELF ON THE SHELF FAMILY COOKBOOK

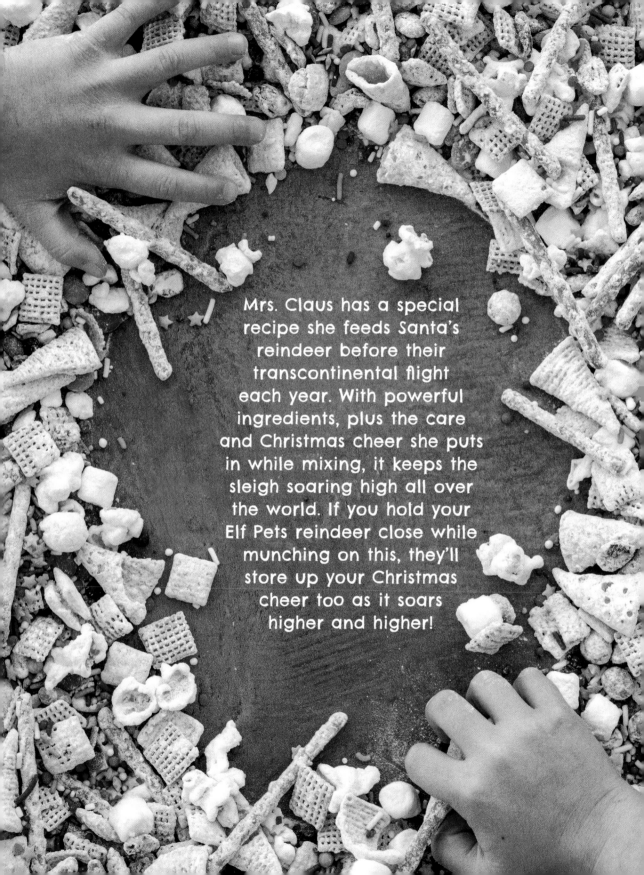

Mrs. Claus has a special recipe she feeds Santa's reindeer before their transcontinental flight each year. With powerful ingredients, plus the care and Christmas cheer she puts in while mixing, it keeps the sleigh soaring high all over the world. If you hold your Elf Pets reindeer close while munching on this, they'll store up your Christmas cheer too as it soars higher and higher!

Reindeer Munch
SNACK MIX

- ☐ 3 cups Rice Chex, Corn Chex, or Chocolate Chex cereal
- ☐ 2 cups popped plain popcorn
- ☐ 2 cups snowflake-shaped pretzels or pretzel sticks
- ☐ 2 cups conical corn snacks, such as Bugles
- ☐ 1 cup dried cranberries or raisins
- ☐ 1 cup mini marshmallows
- ☐ 1 cup red and green candy-coated chocolates, such as M&M's
- ☐ 8 ounces white candy melts
- ☐ 1 cup powdered sugar
- ☐ ½ cup festive sprinkles

1. Line a sheet pan with parchment paper.
2. In a large bowl, stir together the cereal, popcorn, pretzels, corn snacks, cranberries, marshmallows, and candy-coated chocolates.
3. Place the candy melts in a medium microwave-safe bowl. Microwave on high, uncovered, in 30-second increments, stirring in between, until melted and smooth.
4. Pour over the cereal mix, stirring until well coated. Stir in the powdered sugar and sprinkles to coat. Spread in an even layer on the prepared sheet pan.
5. Let set for about 1 hour, then divide into bowls for movie-watching munching. Store the snack mix in an airtight container at room temperature for up to 1 week.

Psst . . . What a joy! What a night! You're helping the reindeer prepare to take flight!

Extraordinary NOORAH Meringues

- ☐ 3 large egg whites, at room temperature (save the yolks for another use!)
- ☐ ½ teaspoon cream of tartar
- ☐ ⅔ cup superfine sugar (see Sweet Shop Secret on page 116)
- ☐ Teal, green, and purple gel-based food colorings

SPECIAL EQUIPMENT

Pastry bag fitted with an open star tip

3 small flat food-safe decorating brushes (optional)

In a faraway world where magic glimmers, Noorah, an ordinary arctic fox, is transformed by the brilliant light of a comet. Now she shines with color from her bright eyes to the tip of her tail and pauses time for Santa's overnight flight around the world. These mini meringues pause overnight too and reveal the beauty of the northern lights the next morning.

1. Position an oven rack in the center of the oven. Preheat the oven to 200°F. Line a sheet pan with parchment paper.

2. To make the meringue, in the bowl of a stand mixer fitted with the whisk attachment (or a large bowl, if using a handheld mixer), whisk together the egg whites and cream of tartar on low speed until frothy, about 1 minute. Increase the speed to medium and continue whisking until thick, about 1 minute more. With the mixer running, slowly add the sugar, letting it gently cascade into the bowl like fresh, falling snow! Continue whisking until stiff, glossy peaks form, about 3 minutes.

3. Place the pastry bag in a tall glass and fold down the sides. Using one of the food-safe decorating brushes (if desired) or the tip of a knife, draw a vertical stripe of teal food coloring inside the bag. With a clean brush or knife, repeat with the green and purple food coloring, spacing the stripes apart.

(recipe continues on page 116)

Meet Noorah!

4. Using a silicone spatula, transfer the meringue to the pastry bag, filling it no more than three-quarters full (work in batches, if necessary). Pipe small dollops of meringue on the prepared sheet pan; you should plan on six rows of 8 meringues each, evenly spaced. Bake for 1 hour, then turn off the oven, but do not open the door! For these cookies to look like the magic of Noorah's tail, they need to remain in the oven overnight. Get all tucked in, and when you wake up, they'll be ready!

MERRY MERINGUES

Bake these meringue variations in a 200°F oven for 1 hour, then turn off the oven and let them cool in the oven for 2 hours.

SNOWPEOPLE: Pipe the meringue into large dollops, then top each with a small dollop. Bake as directed. Once cool, decorate by using a spot of store-bought frosting or icing as "glue" to attach a strip of fruit leather snack, cut lengthwise, for a scarf; black sprinkles for eyes and buttons; and an orange sprinkle nose.

WREATHS: Pipe the meringue into rounds that are 2 inches across. Sprinkle with green sanding sugar before baking.

STARLIGHT CANDY SPIRALS: Paint four strips of red (or green) gel-based food coloring in a pastry bag fitted with a large round tip. Pipe spirals that are 1 inch across, then bake as directed.

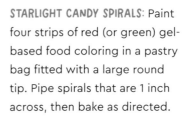

SWEET SHOP SECRET

Superfine sugar is finely ground granulated sugar essential for meringue making since it dissolves faster. You can purchase it or make it by grinding granulated sugar in a blender until powdery!

NOORAH'S STORY IS AS
EXTRAORDINARY AS THE
NORTHERN LIGHTS!

Jolly Holly
POPCORN BALLS

If I had to choose a popcorn snack, say caramel or cheese,
I'd have to say there's just this one for movie night—so, please?
It's tinted red, like Santa's suit, which makes it very jolly,
But if you wish, just tint it green, and "dress it up" like holly.

- ☐ 18 cups (4 microwave bags) plain, unsalted popped popcorn
- ☐ 4 tablespoons (½ stick) unsalted butter, cut into small pieces
- ☐ ¾ cup light corn syrup
- ☐ 1½ cups mini marshmallows
- ☐ 2½ cups powdered sugar
- ☐ 7 to 10 drops red or green gel food coloring
- ☐ 3 tablespoons or more festive sprinkles (optional)
- ☐ Cooking spray

MERRY MIXIFIER MACHINE

1. Line 2 sheet pans with parchment paper.
2. Place the popcorn in a large deep bowl or pot.
3. In a medium saucepan over medium heat, melt the butter. Add 2 tablespoons of water, the corn syrup, marshmallows, and powdered sugar and cook, stirring often, until the mixture is completely melted and comes to a boil, 5 to 7 minutes. Add your choice of food coloring, stirring continuously until incorporated.
4. Immediately pour the hot marshmallow mixture over the popcorn and use a wooden spoon to mix thoroughly to coat, turning your popcorn red. Stir in the sprinkles, if using.
5. When the popcorn is cool enough to handle, spray your clean hands with cooking spray and pack about ½ cup of popcorn into a ball, as if packing a snowball! Place the popcorn ball on one of the prepared sheet pans. Repeat with the remaining popcorn, packing popcorn balls as Santa size or elf size as you wish!

Snow Blizzard CREAM

MAKES 4 SERVINGS

Oh, hello! Last night, this recipe fell right out of the sky and into our arms for you!

- Powdered sugar
- 8 cups clean freshly fallen snow or shaved ice
- One 14-ounce can sweetened condensed milk
- 1 teaspoon pure vanilla extract

FOR TOPPING
- Festive sprinkles
- Chocolate sauce
- Cookies, any kind, or graham crackers, crumbled
- Whipped cream
- Sticky bananas (see page 24)
- Toffee sauce (see page 156), at room temperature
- Cherry compote (see page 167) or candied cherries, such as Maraschino

SPECIAL EQUIPMENT
Shaved ice maker or stand mixer shaved ice attachment (optional)

1. Using a fine-mesh sieve, dust the inside and edges of four serving bowls with powdered sugar—it's a blizzard!
2. Place the snow in a large bowl. Stir in the condensed milk and vanilla until well combined and creamy.
3. Scoop the sweetened snow into the blizzard bowls and top as you wish, perhaps with a giant dollop of whipped cream with sprinkles.

SWEET SHOP SECRET

When collecting fresh snow, look for white, undisturbed snow from a pile above ground level—the less likely it has met with cats, dogs, and woodland creatures! Gently scrape away the top layer and scoop the snow underneath into a large bowl or pot. Freeze or keep outside until ready to use.

Brrrrrr!

CHAPTER 4

SCOUT ELF
Dinner
Takeover

MAC 'N' CHEESE BITES

We made dinner plans when you slipped into slumber last night! Feast your peepers on this velvety bowl of mac 'n' cheese that we shaped into nuggets for nibbling.

- ☐ Cooking spray
- ☐ Kosher salt
- ☐ 2 cups uncooked elbow macaroni or small pasta shells
- ☐ 1 tablespoon unsalted butter, plus more for greasing
- ☐ 1 tablespoon all-purpose flour
- ☐ 1½ cups whole milk
- ☐ Pinch of freshly ground black pepper
- ☐ 2½ cups shredded Cheddar, Pepper Jack, or other cheese
- ☐ Chili powder

SPECIAL EQUIPMENT
Two 12-cup mini muffin tins, or one 24-cup mini muffin tin

1. Preheat the oven to 350°F. Grease the muffin tin cups with cooking spray.
2. Bring a pot of lightly salted water to a boil. Add the macaroni and cook for 5 minutes, until slightly undercooked. Drain and set aside.
3. In a medium saucepan set over medium heat, melt the 1 tablespoon of butter. Whisk in the flour until smooth, about 10 seconds. Slowly add the milk, ½ teaspoon salt, and the pepper and whisk to combine. Raise the heat to medium-high and add 2 cups of the cheese. Cook, whisking constantly, until the mixture thickens into a smooth cheese sauce, about 2 minutes. Remove from the heat. Using a wooden spoon, stir the macaroni into the sauce until well coated.
4. Divide the remaining ½ cup cheese among the muffin tin cups, about 1 teaspoon per cup. Fill each cup with about 2 tablespoons of macaroni and cheese—use the back of the spoon or your clean fingers to pack it down. Top each with a sprinkle of chili powder.
5. Bake until bubbling, 10 minutes, then rotate the pan and continue baking until the mac 'n' cheese cups are firm and the tops are browned, about 5 minutes more. Cool on a wire rack for 10 minutes. Use a butter knife to gently loosen the mini macs from the pan before serving.

SCOUT ELF FAVORITES

WHAT'S A SCOUT ELF'S FAVORITE SPICE?
"CHILLY" POWDER

FAVORITE PASTA?
ELF-ABET

FAVORITE CHEESE?
CHEER-DAR

FAVORITE WAY TO EAT THEM ALL?
ELF-RESCO (UNDER THE NORTH POLE SKY!)

Tiny TACO PARTY

During our afternoon siesta, we were dreaming of tacos with drizzles of snow-white cream and fresh avocados. We woke up with a plan—a post-siesta fiesta! We measured and mixed, squeezed and stirred, drizzled and . . . oh, what a delight! Want a bite?

FOR THE CREMA
- ☐ ¼ cup sour cream
- ☐ ¼ cup heavy cream
- ☐ ¼ teaspoon kosher salt
- ☐ 1 teaspoon freshly squeezed lime juice

FOR THE TINY TACOS
- ☐ 2 tablespoons olive oil
- ☐ 1 pound ground chicken or turkey
- ☐ ½ pound ground chorizo
- ☐ 2 teaspoons chili powder
- ☐ 1 tablespoon ground cumin
- ☐ 1 teaspoon kosher salt
- ☐ ½ teaspoon freshly ground black pepper
- ☐ One 11-ounce package mini (street taco) flour tortillas
- ☐ ¼ cup shredded Cheddar cheese
- ☐ ½ cup chopped fresh cilantro
- ☐ Lime wedges
- ☐ Avocado slices

1. Preheat the oven to 200°F. Line a sheet pan with parchment paper.
2. Make the crema: In a small bowl, stir together the sour cream, heavy cream, salt, and lime juice. Cover and refrigerate until ready to use.
3. Make the tacos: Heat the olive oil in a large nonstick skillet over medium-high heat. When the oil is shimmering, add the chicken, chorizo, chili powder, cumin, salt, and pepper and cook, stirring, until no pink parts of the chicken or chorizo remain, about 8 minutes.
4. Place the tortillas on the prepared sheet pan. Top each with a sprinkle of cheese and warm until the cheese melts, 2 to 3 minutes.
5. Remove the tortillas from the oven. Spoon about 1½ tablespoons of the prepared filling over each tortilla, then carefully fold them closed to make tacos. Drizzle some crema over the top and garnish with cilantro. Serve with lime wedges and sliced avocado.

Bitty BURGER BITES

We made you bitty burgers—a dozen (not a ton!).
Now take a bite and you will taste your burger in the bun.
We tucked them in with bits of cheese—placed pickles on their heads.
It's as if our bitty burgers are tucked inside bun-beds.

- ☐ 1 pound ground beef
- ☐ 2 tablespoons Worcestershire sauce
- ☐ ½ teaspoon garlic powder
- ☐ ½ teaspoon kosher salt
- ☐ ½ teaspoon freshly ground black pepper
- ☐ 2 teaspoons olive oil
- ☐ All-purpose flour
- ☐ One 16-ounce ball store-bought pizza dough, at room temperature
- ☐ 3 ounces Cheddar cheese, cut into 12 cubes
- ☐ 1 large egg, lightly beaten
- ☐ Sesame seeds
- ☐ 12 mini gherkin pickles
- ☐ 12 cherry tomatoes
- ☐ Ketchup, for dipping

SPECIAL EQUIPMENT
12 festive toothpicks

1. Preheat the oven to 375°F. Set out a wire cooling rack with a sheet of parchment paper underneath for easy cleanup. Line a sheet pan with parchment paper and set aside.

2. In a medium bowl, combine the beef, Worcestershire sauce, garlic powder, salt, and pepper. Using your clean hands, form 12 bitty burger patties about 1 inch thick. Wash your hands!

3. Heat the olive oil in a large nonstick skillet over medium heat. When the oil is shimmering, add the burgers. Cook for 2 minutes on one side. Flip and continue cooking on the other side, 2 minutes more—the burgers will be browned on the outside and medium-rare in the center. Transfer the burgers to the prepared wire rack and allow to rest for 10 minutes.

4. Lightly flour a clean work surface and turn out the pizza dough. Using your clean hands, pinch off 12 equal-size pieces dough (about 1½ ounces each). Roll each portion into a soft ball. Using the palm of your hand, flatten each ball into a circle.

5. Place a bitty burger in the center of each dough ball, then top with a cheese cube. Gather the dough over the burger and pinch to seal closed. Place on the prepared sheet pan, seam side down.

6. Brush the tops of the dough with the egg and sprinkle generously with sesame seeds. Bake until lightly golden, 10 minutes. Rotate the pan and continue baking, until the seeds are toasted and the burger is cooked through, 8 minutes more. Use a toothpick to skewer a pickle and a tomato through the top of the bun. Take your burger for a dip in ketchup, then take a bitty bite!

Crust us, They're Delicious!

We thought of making you pepperoni pizza for dinner, but at the last minute came up with something a bit more "elf-bitious." Presenting mini sweetzas—a petite treat that's fun to eat!

- ☐ Cooking spray
- ☐ All-purpose flour
- ☐ One 16-ounce ball store-bought pizza dough, at room temperature
- ☐ 1 teaspoon sugar
- ☐ ½ teaspoon ground cinnamon
- ☐ 1 tablespoon melted unsalted butter
- ☐ Scout Elf sweet pizza toppings (suggestions below)

1. Preheat the oven to 475°F. Grease a sheet pan with cooking spray.
2. Lightly flour a clean work surface and turn the pizza dough out. Using your clean hands, pinch off 12 equal-size pieces of dough (about 1½ ounces each). Roll each portion into a soft ball. Using the palm of your hand, flatten each ball into a round. Place it on the prepared sheet pan.
3. In a small bowl, combine the sugar and cinnamon. Brush the tops of the dough with melted butter and sprinkle on the cinnamon sugar.
4. Bake until the house smells of cinnamon and the crusts are lightly browned, about 10 minutes. Transfer to a wire rack to cool.
5. When the crusts are cool enough to handle, create your choice of Scout Elf petite sweetzas—try them all!

CHRISTMAS COOKIE
Cookie butter spread (such as Biscoff), festive sprinkles, Golden Cheer (page 25), crushed cookies

S'MORES
Chocolate hazelnut spread, marshmallow cream, crushed graham crackers

FUDGEBERRY
Hot fudge sauce, chopped strawberries, whipped cream

FESTIVE FRUITY
Lemon curd, blueberries, shredded coconut

Fudgeberry

Christmas Cookie

Festive Fruity

S'mores

Elf-abet
TOMATO SOUP

MAKES 6 SERVINGS

- ☐ 4 tablespoons (½ stick) unsalted butter
- ☐ 1 small yellow onion, finely chopped
- ☐ 1 celery stalk, finely chopped
- ☐ 2 garlic cloves, minced
- ☐ One 28-ounce can tomato purée
- ☐ 4 cups (1 quart) vegetable or chicken broth
- ☐ 2 teaspoons kosher salt
- ☐ Pinch of freshly ground black pepper
- ☐ ½ cup heavy cream
- ☐ 1 cup uncooked alphabet letters pasta

Sweets bring smiles and power our miles. However, Santa and Mrs. Claus also grow colorful fruits and vegetables at the North Pole—in a red and "green house," of course! Tomatoes and other fruits and veggies give us extra energy for our merrymaking missions and help us keep a well-balanced diet. We added elf-abet pasta to our favorite tomato soup to bring A+ fun to your bowl!

1. In a large soup pot over medium heat, melt the butter. Add the onion and celery and cook until softened, 5 to 7 minutes, stirring often. Add the garlic and cook, stirring until fragrant, about 1 minute.

2. Add the tomato purée, broth, salt, and pepper. Increase the heat to high and bring to a boil. Reduce the heat to low, partially cover with the lid, and simmer, stirring now and then, until the soup reduces in volume by about one-third, 20 to 25 minutes. Stir in the cream and continue cooking 5 minutes more for the flavors to meld.

3. Add the pasta and continue simmering until the pasta is cooked, according to the directions on the package.

4. Divide among bowls for serving right away. See if you can spot a merry message!

Mini Pancake & Waffle
STACK-TACULARS

- One 40-count box (14.1 ounces) store-bought frozen mini pancakes, plain or flavored
- One 40-count box (10.9 ounces) store-bought frozen waffles, plain or flavored
- Assorted spreads, sauces, and dips, such as hazelnut spread, cookie spread, peanut butter, chocolate sauce, flavored yogurt, Marshmallow Cream Dip (page 93), or toffee sauce (see page 156)
- Assorted syrups, such as maple, blueberry, or raspberry
- Assorted fresh fruit, such as blueberries, raspberries, strawberries, diced pineapple, bananas, or sticky bananas (see page 24), or fruit jams, marmalades, butters, or curds
- Plain or flavored whipped dairy topping, such as strawberry, marshmallow, or chocolate
- Assorted toppers, such as sprinkles, mini baking chips, shredded coconut, granola, powdered sugar, cocoa powder, or Golden Cheer (page 25)

Our mission is to spread Christmas cheer right up until the magical moment Santa stacks presents under your tree—and beyond! A stack of mini pancakes and waffles with yummy sauces, dips, and toppers is sure to keep spirits high any time of year. It's a syrup-remely fun breakfast-for-dinner delight!

1. Prepare the frozen mini pancakes and waffles according to the directions on the packages.
2. Assemble the charcuterie board: Place the spreads, sauces, dips, syrups, fruit, fruit jams, marmalades, butters, and curds in assorted individual bowls. Arrange them on the periphery of the board. Place the prepared mini pancakes and waffles in the center. Place whipped topping and toppers in small bowls (or leave the whipped topping in the canisters for squirting), filling in empty spaces.
3. Make mini stacks on individual plates by spreading, dotting, dipping, and topping the pancakes and waffles as desired, using the toothpicks to hold them together.

SPECIAL EQUIPMENT

Assorted small bowls

Large charcuterie board or serving platter

Festive toothpicks

THE ELF ON THE SHELF FAMILY COOKBOOK

Loading Christmas Spirit...

SWEET SHOP SECRET

There are countless ways to make mini stack-taculars. Here are some of our favorite combos.

- Peanut butter, jam, granola, whipped topping

- Marshmallow Cream Dip (page 93), mini chips, cocoa powder

- Flavored yogurt, diced pineapple, shredded coconut

- Hazelnut spread, raspberries, whipped topping

- Pure maple syrup or flavored pancake syrup, blueberries, powdered sugar

- Cookie spread, bananas, Golden Cheer (page 25)

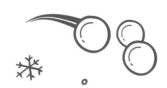

MAKES A STOCKPILE OF ELF-SIZE SNOWBALLS

"Time to duck!" Santa shouts, when snowballs fly about.
At a speed of four per second, you'd duck too, no doubt!
Once the battle's fought and won,
Try your hand at making some.
Sno'ordinary snowballs—no!
They're peanut-snowball-butter dough!

- ☐ 1 cup powdered sugar
- ☐ ½ cup creamy peanut butter
- ☐ ¼ cup honey
- ☐ ⅔ cup dry whole milk powder

1. Place the powdered sugar in a medium bowl.
2. In another medium bowl, use a silicone spatula to stir together the peanut butter and honey. Add the milk powder in three additions, thoroughly stirring to incorporate the powder after each addition, until a thick dough forms.
3. Using your clean hands, pinch off chickpea-size bits of dough and roll them into balls—if the dough is crumbly, squeeze, then roll. As you work, drop the balls in the bowl with the powdered sugar and toss to coat. Place these "snowballs" on a plate for your Scout Elves to replenish their stockpile. Continue rolling until you have used up all the dough.

THE ELF ON THE SHELF FAMILY COOKBOOK

PEANUT BUTTER
SNOWBALL
PERFECTION!!

Colossal COOK!E

Oh no! Our magical shrinking machine malfunctioned and reversed its effects. Instead of a cascade of cute mini cookies covering your counter, there's a colossal surprise. Oh, well! At least there's enough to share!

- ☐ All-purpose flour
- ☐ Two 16-ounce packages ready-to-bake chocolate chip cookie dough
- ☐ ½ cup flavored baking chips, such as chocolate, peanut butter, or hot cocoa and marshmallow
- ☐ ¼ cup mini candy-coated chocolates, such as M&M's minis
- ☐ Ice cream (optional)

1. Position an oven rack in the center of the oven. Preheat the oven to 350°F. Line a sheet pan with parchment paper.
2. Lightly dust a work surface with flour. Roll one of the packaged cookie doughs into a large ball. Using the palms of your clean hands, flatten it into a round about 6½ inches in diameter. Place the cookie circle in the center of the prepared sheet pan. Scatter the baking chips over the top and gently press them into the dough.
3. Dust your work surface with more flour, if needed. Make a second cookie round with the remaining package of dough. Place this cookie round on top of the first cookie round. Use your fingers to pinch the rounds together, sealing the edges shut. Gently press the candy-coated chocolates into the top of the dough.
4. Bake until the edges of the cookie are golden brown and the center is set, about 35 minutes—it will grow to a colossal cookie, about 11 inches in diameter!
5. Let the cookie cool for 20 minutes, then transfer it to a wire cooling rack to cool completely.
6. To serve, cut the cookie into wedges, and top with a scoop of ice cream, if you wish!

That's YETI-size!

CHAPTER 5

CHRISTMAS AROUND THE WORLD

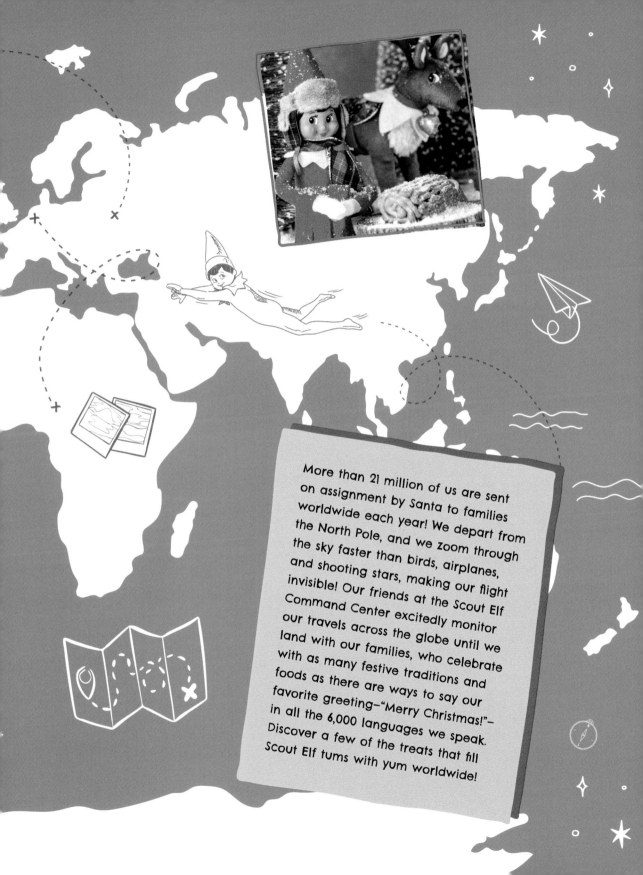

More than 21 million of us are sent on assignment by Santa to families worldwide each year! We depart from the North Pole, and we zoom through the sky faster than birds, airplanes, and shooting stars, making our flight invisible! Our friends at the Scout Elf Command Center excitedly monitor our travels across the globe until we land with our families, who celebrate with as many festive traditions and foods as there are ways to say our favorite greeting—"Merry Christmas!"—in all the 6,000 languages we speak. Discover a few of the treats that fill Scout Elf tums with yum worldwide!

The Sweetest SHOP

We get a festive feeling when we taste the sweets and cookies at Mrs. Claus' Sweet Shop. Here's hoping you feel as cheery as we do with a sweet shop of your own to decorate!

Sweet Shop Elves'
DECORATING IDEAS

FOR THE SWEET SHOP
- ☐ 1 store-bought gingerbread house kit (includes four walls, roof, and gingerbread base)
- ☐ 1 recipe Mrs. Claus' Royal Icing (page 10)

SPECIAL EQUIPMENT

Large cutting board or serving tray

Pastry bag fitted with large round tip

12-cup muffin tin

Below are suggested items from the stock of goodies that we talk about and make in this book. Or browse the aisles at your favorite grocery store as you go on a holiday hunt for candies to spark your inspiration—it will be the sweetest shop(ping) ever!

ROOF

- Use festive cereal, yogurt-covered raisins, or sliced almonds, for a gravel rooftop.
- Apply sticks of gum, for shingles.
- Dust waffle pretzels with powdered sugar, for a snowy tin roof.
- Try fruit leather snack strips, for a colorful roof siding.
- Apply a thick layer of Mrs. Claus' Royal Icing (page 10), for a snow-covered North Pole Sweet Shop. Pipe icicles by holding the bag upward and pressing it against the edge of the roof. Squeeze a mound of icing, then pull away fast.
- Use pretzel rods, for a log cabin look.
- Attach starlight candies or starlight candy spirals (see page 116), for a peppermint roof.

SIDING, DOOR, AND WINDOWS

- Try peppermint sticks, for lining the corners of the cottage or the door as porch pillars.
- Pipe a thread of icing and attach chocolate-coated candies (like M&M's), chewy candy bites, or small jelly beans, for string lights.
- Pipe icing on a round butter cookie and decorate with green sprinkles, for a wreath or attach a Merry Meringue Wreath (page 116).
- Use colored candy melts, for roof and siding texture.
- Attach Elf-Size Doughnut Delights! (page 55), for fanciful fun.
- Use round butter cookies or vanilla wafer cookies, halved and attached back-to-back, for easy window shutters.

WALKWAY AND SURROUNDING DECOR

Create a walkway by piping a 3-inch-wide pathway from the edge of the base to the doorway and cover with such items as:

- Shredded coconut or white and snowflake sprinkles, for snow.
- Crushed chocolate sandwich cookies, for gravel.
- Gummy fruits or gumdrops, for a candy lane.

Choose items such as trees and sleds from Decked-Out Dippers (page 80) to place around your Sweet Shop and add a snowperson meringue (see page 116) or two.

It's "snow" sweet!

Sweet Shop
DIRECTIONS

1. Before you begin, read the Sweet Shop Elves' Decorating Ideas above.
2. Assemble the house according to the directions on the package on a sturdy display base, such as a large cutting board or serving tray. Fill the pastry bag halfway with icing. Expect to use a generous 1½ to 2 cups icing for assembly. Let dry completely before decorating, about 1 hour.
3. Place candies, nuts, cereal, and other items in the muffin tin cups to keep them organized and within easy reach.
4. Decorate, using the remaining 4 to 4½ cups icing to attach candy and goodies, to pipe a snowy walkway, or to layer a thick, fluffy snow-covered roof, just like on the Sweet Shop back at the North Pole.

SWEET SHOP SECRET
Mini Graham Cracker Cottage

- ☐ 2 graham cracker sheets, halved (4 squares)
- ☐ Mrs. Claus' Royal Icing (page 10) or store-bought icing
- ☐ Assorted candies (see pages 150–151 for suggestions)

1. "Glue" together two graham cracker squares with royal icing to create a strong base.
2. Line the bottom edge of each remaining square with icing and attach to the base, angling the squares so they join at the top. Pipe icing at their meeting point to "glue" them together. Decorate as you wish.

Our Favorite Greeting
IN ANY LANGUAGE

Here's what we hear from some of our listening and watching spots around the world each season. Can you guess the greeting?
(Hint: Merry _____!)

**Afrikaans –
Geseënde Kersfees!**

**Mandarin Chinese –
Shèngdàn jié kuàilè!**

**Dutch –
Vrolijk Kerstfeest!**

**French –
Joyeux Noël!**

**Filipino –
Maligayang Pasko!**

THE ELF ON THE SHELF FAMILY COOKBOOK

German –
Frohe Weihnachten!

Hausa –
Barka da Kirsimeti

Irish (Gaelic) –
Nollaig Shona duit!

Italian –
Buon Natale!

Japanese –
Merii Kurisumasu!

Latvian –
Priecīgus Ziemassvētkus!

Portuguese –
Feliz Natal!

Spanish –
Feliz Navidad!

Swahili –
Krismasi Njema!

Swiss German –
Schöni Wiehnachte!

Welsh –
Nadolig Llawen!

Yoruba –
Ikini Ọdon Keresimesi!

Sticky Toffee Pudding MUG CAKE

MAKES 1 MUG CAKE

Our Scout Elf friend Jerry-O, on assignment in the United Kingdom, told us all about this gooey, traditional Christmas cake concoction rich with dates and toffee that he thinks is the bees' knees! We were gobsmacked when he told us how to make a single serving in a mug as a late-night snack. We did—and now we're stuffed!

FOR THE CAKE

- ☐ 6 dates, pitted and finely chopped
- ☐ ¼ teaspoon baking soda
- ☐ ¼ cup boiling water
- ☐ 1 large egg
- ☐ 2 tablespoons dark brown sugar
- ☐ ¼ teaspoon pure vanilla extract
- ☐ 4 tablespoons all-purpose flour
- ☐ Pinch of kosher salt

FOR THE TOFFEE SAUCE

- ☐ 2 tablespoons butter
- ☐ ¼ cup packed dark brown sugar
- ☐ 2 tablespoons heavy cream, plus more for topping

1. Make the cake: Place the dates in an 8-ounce mug. Sprinkle with the baking soda, then pour in the boiling water. Let sit for 5 minutes to activate the baking soda and soften the dates.
2. Add the egg, brown sugar, and vanilla and stir to combine. Add the flour and salt and stir to combine.
3. Place the mug in the microwave and cook, uncovered, on high, until the cake rises and sets, 1½ to 2 minutes. Let cool for 1 to 2 minutes.
4. Make the sauce: Place the butter in a small microwave-safe bowl. Melt, uncovered, on high, 15 to 20 seconds. Add the brown sugar and cream and whisk to combine. Return the bowl to the microwave and microwave in 30-second increments, stirring in between, until melted and smooth. Pour the sauce over the cake, add a dollop of cream, and enjoy.

Panettone TRUFFLES

MAKES 16 TO 18 TRUFFLES

Our Scout Elf friend *Tartufo* sent us this Christmas recipe from his Italian family's nonna. These little truffles are made with a sweet, fruit-studded Christmas bread called panettone!

Prendi del panettone, sbriciolalo, e mescolalo con formaggio cremoso. Forma delle palline di tartufo, immergile nel cioccolato fuso e cospargile con glitter commestibile! Buon Natale.

We rewrote her directions for you below!

- ☐ 12 ounces panettone bread, torn
- ☐ 6 ounces cream cheese, at room temperature
- ☐ 2 cups white chocolate chips
- ☐ 2 tablespoons coconut oil
- ☐ Red and green edible glitter

1. Line a sheet pan with parchment paper.
2. Add the torn panettone pieces to the bowl of a food processor and pulse ten to twelve times, until finely crumbed.
3. In a medium bowl, combine the panettone crumbs and cream cheese and stir until a smooth dough forms. Using your clean hands, roll the dough into walnut-size balls and place them on the prepared sheet pan. The dough should yield 16 to 18 balls. Refrigerate for 20 minutes before dipping.
4. Combine the baking chips and coconut oil in a medium microwave-safe bowl. Microwave on high, uncovered, in 30-second increments, stirring in between, until melted and smooth, about *due minuti* (2 minutes) total. Set aside.
5. Working with 1 ball at a time, drop it in the chocolate. Use a spoon to gently coat, then roll the ball onto a fork to lift it out. Gently tap the fork handle against the rim of the bowl to remove any excess chocolate. Roll the ball off the fork onto the prepared sheet pan. Repeat with the remaining balls.
6. Sprinkle the balls with red and green glitter. Refrigerate until the chocolate is set, about 20 minutes, before enjoying. Store in an airtight container at room temperature for 2 days or in the refrigerator for up to 1 week.

YULE LOVE THIS LOG

Here's a recipe for a très elftastic French Christmas cake called bûche de Noël, which looks like a woodsy log. We know yule love to make and eat it, especially for a tree-trimming celebration! In France, our Scout Elf friends Bois and Étincelle make mini logs for thems-elves. To see how they do it, turn to the *Sweet Shop Secret* on page 163 for their Bûche de Noël Nibbles! recipe.

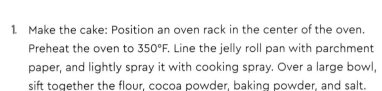

FOR THE SPONGE CAKE

- ☐ Cooking spray
- ☐ ¾ cup all-purpose flour
- ☐ ¼ cup unsweetened cocoa powder
- ☐ 1 teaspoon baking powder
- ☐ ¼ teaspoon kosher salt
- ☐ 5 large eggs, at room temperature
- ☐ ¾ cup granulated sugar
- ☐ Powdered sugar

FOR THE WHIPPED CREAM FILLING

- ☐ 1¼ cups cold heavy cream
- ☐ ⅓ cup powdered sugar
- ☐ ½ teaspoon pure vanilla extract

FOR DECORATING

- ☐ 4 cups chocolate buttercream (see page 000) or store-bought frosting
- ☐ 4 spearmint-leaf candies
- ☐ 3 red gumdrop candies
- ☐ Powdered sugar (optional)

SPECIAL EQUIPMENT

Rimmed jelly roll pan (15.5 × 10.5 inches)

Toothpick

Large kitchen towel

Festive serving platter

1. Make the cake: Position an oven rack in the center of the oven. Preheat the oven to 350°F. Line the jelly roll pan with parchment paper, and lightly spray it with cooking spray. Over a large bowl, sift together the flour, cocoa powder, baking powder, and salt. Whisk to combine and set aside.

2. In the bowl of a stand mixer fitted with the whisk attachment (or another large bowl, if using a handheld mixer), whisk the eggs on low speed, about 1 minute. Add the granulated sugar slowly, letting it cascade into the bowl like fresh, falling snow! Increase the speed to medium and continue whisking until thick and fluffy, 6 to 7 minutes. Stop the mixer and remove the bowl.

3. Add half of the flour mixture to the bowl. Use a silicone spatula to gently fold in the flour to combine. Repeat with the remaining flour mixture, gently folding until there are no streaks of flour. The batter should still be airy.

4. Gently spread the batter evenly in the prepared pan. Bake for 5 minutes. Rotate the pan, and continue baking until the house smells like chocolate, the cake springs back when you touch it, and the toothpick inserted in the center comes out clean, about 2 minutes more. Remove from the oven and cool slightly, about 5 minutes. It must still be warm to roll properly.

5. Place the towel on a clean work surface and use a fine-mesh sieve to coat with a dusting of powdered sugar. This will prevent the cake from sticking to the towel.

6. Use a butter knife to loosen the edges of the still-warm cake. Invert the cake onto the prepared towel and remove the parchment paper. With the long side of the cake facing you, tightly roll the cake away from you, in the towel, forming a log. Place the towel-wrapped cake log on a wire cooling rack to cool completely, about 1 hour.

7. Meanwhile, make the filling: In the bowl of a stand mixer fitted with the whisk attachment (or a large bowl, if using a handheld mixer), whisk the cream on low speed, about 1 minute. Slowly add the powdered sugar and vanilla, gradually increasing the speed to medium-high, whisking until soft peaks form, about 1 minute. Refrigerate until ready to use.

8. Fill the cake: Slowly unroll the log onto a large cutting board—it won't be perfectly flat, and that's okay. Spread the whipped cream evenly across the cake and reroll it (without the towel!). Transfer the cream-filled log to the serving platter and refrigerate for 15 minutes.

9. To decorate: Using the back of a large spoon, swirl and swoop 3 cups of the chocolate buttercream over the top, sides, and front of the cake, creating a woodsy bark texture. Decorate the top of the log with a candy holly leaf (4 spearmint-leaf candies with 3 red gumdrops in the center). Finish with a dusting of powdered sugar, if you wish.

10. Reserve the remaining 1 cup buttercream in an airtight container in the refrigerator for up to 1 week. Or use it immediately for Bûche de Noël Nibbles!

SWEET SHOP SECRET
Bûche de Noël Nibbles!
On Christmas Eve in France, children fill their shoes with carrots and leave them by the fireplace as a treat for Santa's donkey, Mistletoe! Scout Elves in France love to gather round mini Yule logs.

Make elf-size Yule logs by using a small spoon to frost Swiss roll snack cakes with buttercream. Decorate as you wish!

Mexican Hot Chocolate
CANDIED NUTS

Our *Scout Elf* friend Elfa Eduarda de las Estrellas tells us that these spicy candied nuts are stupendous on their own, hanging out with pancakes, or in a mix with popcorn!

- ☐ 1 large egg white
- ☐ 4½ cups unsalted nuts, such as peanuts, pecans, almonds, or a combo
- ☐ 2 tablespoons Mrs. Claus' Santa-Size Batch of Cocoa Mix (page 40) or store-bought mix
- ☐ 2 teaspoons ground cinnamon
- ☐ ¼ teaspoon ground nutmeg
- ☐ ¼ teaspoon ground cayenne
- ☐ ¼ teaspoon ground allspice
- ☐ ½ cup sugar
- ☐ ¼ teaspoon kosher salt

1. Position two oven racks, evenly spaced, in the center of the oven. Preheat the oven to 300°F. Line a sheet pan with aluminum foil.
2. In a large bowl, whisk the egg white with 1 tablespoon of water until frothy. Add the nuts and toss until well coated. Add the cocoa, cinnamon, nutmeg, cayenne, allspice, sugar, and salt, and toss to coat.
3. Spread the nuts in an even layer on the prepared sheet pan. Bake until the coating is crujiente (crunchy), tossing halfway through, about 20 minutes. Transfer to a wire rack to cool before snacking.

"Santa, Stop Here!" TRIFLE

FOR THE "NOSE LIKE A CHERRY" COMPOTE

- ☐ Two 16-ounce bags frozen cherries
- ☐ 2 tablespoons granulated sugar
- ☐ Pinch of kosher salt

FOR THE "CHIMNEY SOOT" CHOCOLATE PUDDING

- ☐ One 3.9-ounce box instant chocolate pudding and pie filling
- ☐ 2 cups whole milk

FOR THE "FRESHLY FALLEN SNOW" CREAM

- ☐ 4 cups (2 pints) cold heavy cream
- ☐ 1 cup powdered sugar, plus more for dusting
- ☐ 2 teaspoons pure vanilla extract

FOR ASSEMBLY

- ☐ One 11.5-ounce all-butter pound cake loaf, cut into 12 slices, then halved for a total of 24 slices (these are your "rooftop shingles")
- ☐ 12 chocolate wafer cookies, finely crumbed (about ¾ cup)

SPECIAL EQUIPMENT
2½- to 3-quart-capacity glass bowl or trifle bowl

When Christmas arrives in Australia, it's their summer season! Our Scout Elf friend Eucalyptus Ellie told us kids wish for snow in the hope that Santa can still stop at their house. (He can!) It gave us the elftastic idea to show you how to make a wintry, joyful version of a traditional Australian trifle—as an ode to one of Santa's first Christmas Eve stops!

1. Make the compote: In a medium saucepan, combine the cherries, granulated sugar, salt, and ¼ cup water. Bring to a boil over medium-high heat and cook, stirring often, until the mixture reduces and thickens, about 12 minutes. Remove from the heat and let cool completely.

2. Make the pudding: In a medium bowl, whisk together the pudding and milk. Set aside to thicken, about 5 minutes.

3. Make the cream: In the bowl of a stand mixer fitted with the whisk attachment (or a large bowl, if using a handheld mixer), whisk the cream on low speed, about 1 minute. Slowly add the powdered sugar and vanilla, gradually increasing the speed to medium-high and beating until soft peaks form, about 1 minute. Set aside.

4. Assemble the trifle: Spoon ½ cup of the cherry compote on the bottom of the bowl. "Shingle" 6 cake squares over the filling, going around the edges of the bowl and filling in the middle. Spoon about ½ cup of the pudding over the cake and spread it out evenly. Sprinkle some of the cookie crumbs over the pudding, to cover. Spoon about ½ cup of the whipped cream over the cookies and spread evenly.

5. Repeat the layering process, creating two more layers with the remaining compote, cake, pudding, cookie crumbs, and cream as the final layer.

6. Cover the trifle with plastic wrap and refrigerate for at least 6 hours for the cake to soften and the flavors to meld.

7. Add "Santa, stop here!" toppers: Before serving, decorate the top with a mini gingerbread house, a tree truffle, or other holiday cookies enticing Santa to "stop here!"

DEPARTURE LETTER

Dear Friend,

Our time together, as we know, is drawing to a close.
But we're leaving with a joy that fills us—cap to toes!
We'll trail behind our boss's sleigh when time comes to depart.
We hope you feel our love for you, nestled in your heart.

We'll treasure all the time we shared—baking, laughing, cooking!
(Sorry if we made some mayhem while you weren't looking.)
We hope you learned a tip or two while reading through each chapter,
But we thought you'd like to know a bit of what comes after.

When we get home, Santa needs our help—"Every Elf on deck!"
For North Pole upgrades, projects . . . and the reindeer? We will check!
Relaxation and a meal—fresh oats and favorite munch.
(Guess who's in charge of making sure they eat a proper lunch!?)

We hope you'll write throughout the year and tell us all your news.
Perhaps invite us back for special visits—if you choose!
Until next time, we thank you much for sharing home 'n' shelves,

We'll count the days until next Christmas . . .

Love,

Your Loyal Scout Elf Pals

we will see you NEXT YEAR!

SOME KITCHEN SINK INGREDIENTS YOU MIGHT FIND

- ☐ Baking chips, such as butterscotch, chocolate, or white
- ☐ Chocolate-covered cherries
- ☐ Dates
- ☐ Dried cranberries
- ☐ The Elf on the Shelf cereal or other favorite cereal
- ☐ Festive sprinkles
- ☐ Graham crackers or mini bear grahams
- ☐ Mini candy-coated chocolates
- ☐ Mini marshmallows
- ☐ Mini candy bars
- ☐ Nonpareils
- ☐ Nuts, such as peanuts, walnuts, or pecans
- ☐ Potato chips
- ☐ Raisins
- ☐ Shredded coconut
- ☐ Pretzels
- ☐ Toffee bits

FOR THE COOKIE DOUGH

- ☐ 2¾ cups all-purpose flour
- ☐ 1 teaspoon baking powder
- ☐ ½ teaspoon kosher salt
- ☐ ½ pound (2 sticks) unsalted butter, melted
- ☐ 1 cup sugar
- ☐ 2 large eggs
- ☐ 1 teaspoon pure vanilla extract

1. Line 2 sheet pans with parchment paper.
2. Prep the kitchen sink ingredients: Crush dry ingredients such as nuts, pretzels, cereal, and/or chips. Chop mini candy bars. Create a special combo of ingredients totaling 4 cups—making sure to include 1½ cups of your choice flavor baking chips, for gooey goodness.
3. Make the cookie dough: In a large bowl, whisk together the flour, baking powder, and salt.
4. In the bowl of a stand mixer fitted with the paddle attachment (or another large bowl, if using a handheld mixer), beat together the butter and sugar on medium speed until smooth, about 30 seconds. Add the eggs and vanilla, then mix on low speed until smooth, about 30 seconds more.
5. Add the flour mixture to the butter mixture and continue to mix on low speed, about 30 seconds. Stop and scrape down the sides of the bowl, then continue mixing until a dough forms, about 30 seconds more.
6. Using a wooden spoon or spatula, fold in the 4 cups of surprise ingredients, making sure to scrape up any finely crushed ingredients that may fall to the bottom of the bowl.
7. Drop about 2 tablespoons of dough at a time onto the prepared sheet pans, spacing them about 2 inches apart. Refrigerate until firm, 20 to 30 minutes.
8. Position two oven racks, evenly spaced, in the center of the oven. Preheat the oven to 350°F.
9. Bake, switching the pans in the oven halfway through, until the cookies are golden brown at the edges, 20 to 22 minutes. Cool on the pan on a wire rack for 10 minutes, then transfer the cookies directly to the rack to cool.

Loading Christmas Spirit...

Cookie
NAME GENERATOR

This cookie tradition began for the _____ family on _____, 20___

The name of our cookie is:

_____

TO FIND THE NAME OF YOUR COOKIE, START WITH THE FIRST LETTER OF YOUR SCOUT ELF'S NAME . . .

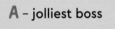

A – jolliest boss	H – St. Nick	O – gregarious	V – shenanigan
B – gooey	I – whimsical	P – deluxe	W – fantastical
C – crunchy	J – fancy-pants	Q – super-duper	X – chippy
D – extravaganzalorious	K – crumbly	R – surprise	Y – fancy-schmancy
E – melty	L – scrumptious	S – tempting	Z – indulgent
F – bold	M – Kris Kringle	T – colossal	
G – tinker	N – decadent	U – divine	

AND ADD YOUR BIRTHDAY MONTH . . .

JANUARY – jing-a-lings

FEBRUARY – bergoopuffs

MARCH – deck-the-hallers

APRIL – chunky-hunky-dunkies

MAY – elfers

JUNE – hodgepodges

JULY – bunch o' stuffers

AUGUST – fiddlestickers

SEPTEMBER – razzlers

OCTOBER – dazzlers

NOVEMBER – kitchen sinkers

DECEMBER – cheer makers

CHAPTER 6
SCOUT ELF SPECIAL RETURNS

Santa called us into his study one day. He was holding a letter in his hand.

I WOULD LIKE ------------------

TO RETURN FOR A SPECIAL VISIT ON -----------

We elf-ed in closer—it was filled out by you! Our eyes grew wide, and we pulled at the collars of our uniforms. We stammered a bit; we were so excited. "Isn't that their birthday?" "Why, yes," Santa said, smiling. And then he pulled out another letter, and another—all requesting permission from you—for Easter, and Christmas in July, and Halloween, and Thanksgiving, and Back to School, and Valentine's Day!

"You may have my permission for a Special Return," he told us, not sugarcoating the news. And we know which one you picked! See you there—we can't wait.

P.S. We have the best boss!

Birthday Berry Pies

- ☐ 2½ cups all-purpose flour, plus more for dusting
- ☐ 2 tablespoons granulated sugar
- ☐ ¾ teaspoon kosher salt
- ☐ ½ pound (2 sticks) cold unsalted butter, cut into ½-inch cubes
- ☐ ¾ cup buttermilk, plus more as needed
- ☐ One 21-ounce can pie filling, such as apple, cherry, or berry medley
- ☐ 1 large egg, beaten with 1 tablespoon water, for an egg wash
- ☐ Sparkling sugar, any color

SPECIAL EQUIPMENT

4-inch round cookie cutter

Hooray! A round of applause on your very special day! In your honor, we brought you these juicy, fruit-filled parcels you can hold in your hands to eat. How old are you? (We're over 1,000 years old—yowza!) Here's how we made these birthday bundles.

1. Generously flour a clean work surface. In a large bowl, whisk together the flour, granulated sugar, and salt. Add the butter and toss to coat in the flour. Using your clean hands, work the butter into the flour mixture, squeezing it between your fingertips, until the mixture resembles coarse bread crumbs.

2. Make a well in the center of the mixture. Add ½ cup of the buttermilk and use your hands to gently incorporate the flour mixture into the buttermilk until combined. Add the remaining ¼ cup buttermilk and gently mix until the dough holds together and there are no dry spots. If needed, add more buttermilk, 1 to 2 tablespoons at a time, and use your hands to achieve a smooth dough.

3. Turn out the dough onto the prepared work surface and use your hands to shape it into a ball. Divide the dough evenly into 2 balls. Wrap each ball in plastic wrap and shape it into a flat disk about ½ inch thick. Refrigerate for 2 hours or up to overnight.

Tiny Elf-Size Pies

4. Line a sheet pan with parchment paper. Lightly flour a work surface. Working with 1 disk at a time, use a rolling pin to roll the disk into a round about 12 inches in diameter and ⅛ inch thick. Using the cookie cutter, cut out dough rounds. Transfer them to the prepared sheet pan. Gather any dough scraps, pat them into a ball, reroll, and cut out more rounds until you have 12 rounds. Repeat the process with the remaining disk so that you have a total of 24 rounds.

5. Brush the outer edges of each round with some of the egg wash. Place about 1 tablespoon of pie filling in the center, leaving a ½-inch border all around (reserve any remaining pie filling for another use). Fold the dough over the filling, creating a half-moon shape. Press the edges closed to seal, then use the tines of a fork to crimp the edges closed. Repeat with the remaining rounds.

6. Brush the top of each pie with the remaining egg wash. Use a sharp knife to gently cut two small slits on the top for air vents. Sprinkle with sparkling sugar.

7. Cover the pies with plastic wrap and refrigerate for 30 minutes before baking.

8. Position an oven rack in the center of the oven. Preheat the oven to 425°F. Remove the wrap from the pies and bake until the tops are golden brown and the filling is bubbly, 15 to 20 minutes. Transfer the pies to a wire rack to cool for at least 10 minutes before serving. The filling will be hot!

Make a wish!

Easter Bunny FUDGE

Happy Easter! Here come treats and eats, bunny ears, and lots of cheers. We brought our favorite version of Mrs. Claus' fudge—hop a square or two into your mouth like we do each time we visit her shop!

- ☐ Cooking spray
- ☐ 2 cups white chocolate chips, or 11 ounces white chocolate bars, chopped
- ☐ 2 teaspoons pure vanilla extract
- ☐ One 14-ounce can sweetened condensed milk
- ☐ ¼ cup mini milk chocolate eggs
- ☐ ¼ cup candy-coated chocolates, such as M&M's, any color
- ☐ ¼ cup assorted jelly beans, any color

SPECIAL EQUIPMENT
8 × 8-inch baking pan

1. Grease the baking pan with cooking spray and line it with parchment paper, allowing a 2-inch overhang on all sides.
2. Fill a medium saucepan with 2 inches of water and bring to a boil over high heat. Lower the heat to a simmer. Set a large heatproof bowl over the saucepan, making sure the bottom doesn't touch the water—it should hover above it. Add the baking chips, vanilla, and condensed milk and stir continuously until the mixture is melted, smooth, and glossy, about 8 minutes. (It will be very thick at first, but keep stirring!) Remove from the heat.
3. Using a silicone spatula, fold the chocolate eggs, candy-coated chocolates, and jelly beans into the mixture. Transfer the mixture to the prepared baking pan. Refrigerate until firm, about 2 hours.
4. Using the parchment paper overhang, lift the fudge out of the pan and place it on a cutting board. Using a sharp knife, cut into about thirty-six 1¼-inch squares. Store the fudge squares in an airtight container at room temperature for up to 1 week.

SWEET SHOP SECRET
Make Easter Magic

STEP 1
Place a whole uncracked egg in a bowl.

STEP 2
Sprinkle with luster dust.

SURPRISE!
When you wake up the next morning, your Scout Elf will have used their magic to turn your egg into a chocolate-covered crème-filled Easter egg treat!

WE POPPED BY FOR *Christmas in July* BROWNIES

MAKES 16
BROWNIE BITES

We flew back for your Christmas in July celebration with a secret ingredient to sprinkle on top of fudgy brownies—and to show you how we're "popping at the seams" with excitement to see you again! Decode our secret message on page 185 to find out what we brought—then search "pop" to bottom to find them in your kitchen.

□ Cooking spray
□ 8 tablespoons (1 stick) unsalted butter, cut into small pieces
□ ¼ cup unsweetened cocoa powder
□ ¾ cup granulated sugar
□ ¼ cup packed light brown sugar
□ 2 large eggs
□ ½ cup all-purpose flour
□ ¼ teaspoon kosher salt
□ 1 teaspoon pure vanilla extract
□ Secret ingredient (see opposite)

SPECIAL EQUIPMENT
8 × 8-inch baking pan

1. Preheat the oven to 350°F. Grease the baking pan with cooking spray and line it with parchment paper, allowing a 2-inch overhang on all sides.

2. Fill a medium saucepan with 2 inches of water and bring to a boil over high heat. Lower the heat to a simmer. Set a medium heatproof bowl over the saucepan, making sure the bottom doesn't touch the water—it should hover above it. Add the butter and cocoa and stir often until smooth.

3. Whisk in the granulated sugar and brown sugar. Add the eggs, one at a time, and whisk until well combined. Stir in the flour, salt, and vanilla until smooth, without any spots of flour. Use a silicone spatula to scrape the batter into the prepared baking pan. Smooth the top.

4. Bake until just set (the middle will jiggle slightly), about 22 minutes. Sprinkle the secret ingredient over the top, then transfer to a wire rack to cool completely. Use the overhang to lift the brownie out of the pan before cutting into sixteen 2-inch brownie bites that "pop"!

Pop, pop, hooray!

THE ELF ON THE SHELF FAMILY COOKBOOK

SECRET INGREDIENT

Two 0.17-ounce packages, any flavor

A - ★ B - 🎄 C - ❄️ D - 🎁 E - 🎅 F - 🔔

G - H - 🧣 I - J - K - 🔔 L - ⚫

M - 🎂 N - 🕯️ O - 🍴 P - 🍭 Q - 🏠 R - 🦌

S - 🍪 T - 🍫 U - 🥓 V - 🔍 W - 🥞 X - 🥣

Y - ⛷️ Z - ⛄

SWEET SHOP SECRET

Instead of the secret ingredient, pop a Santa hat on your brownie bite! Swirl whipped cream on a brownie square and top with an inverted hulled summer-ripe strawberry. Top the strawberry with a dollop of whipped cream for the hat's pom-pom.

spooktacular POTIONS

Create these potions 1-2-3,
for spooky celebrations:

A "witches' brew," a "creature's face,"
a "wormy red creation,"

The tricks to make these creepy drinks
depart from your routine.

But we're here to "stir up fun,"
and "cheers" to Halloween.

- 4 cups (1 quart) chilled white cranberry juice
- 4 cups (1 quart) chilled ginger ale
- 2 drops gel-based black food coloring
- Light corn syrup
- Four 0.17-ounce packages blue Pop Rocks, crushed

Witches' BREW

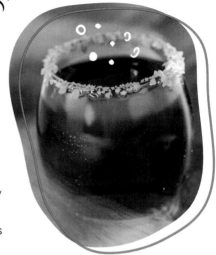

1. In a large pitcher, stir together the juice, ginger ale, and food coloring. Refrigerate until ready to serve.
2. To serve, dip the rims of glasses in corn syrup and then in Pop Rocks. Divide the drink evenly among the glasses. Crackle-cackle.

- 4 cups (1 quart) chilled pineapple juice
- 2 cups chilled orange juice
- 2 cups chilled ginger ale or sparkling water
- Light corn syrup
- Orange sanding sugar
- 8 to 12 large gummy eyeballs, for garnish

SPECIAL EQUIPMENT
4-inch toothpicks

Creature's FACE

1. In a large pitcher, stir together the juices and ginger ale. Refrigerate until ready to serve.
2. To serve, dip the rims of glasses in corn syrup and then in sanding sugar. Divide the drink evenly among the glasses. Thread 2 gummy eyeballs onto a toothpick and set them over each glass. It's alive!

Wormy RED CREATION

- 4 cups (1 quart) chilled cranberry or pomegranate juice
- 4 cups (1 quart) chilled ginger ale or sparkling water
- 3 ounces red candy melts
- 6 to 8 gummy worms

1. In a large pitcher, stir together the juice and ginger ale. Refrigerate until ready to serve.
2. Place the melts in a small microwave-safe bowl. Microwave on high, uncovered, in 30-second increments, stirring in between, until melted and smooth.
3. To serve, dip the rims of glasses in candy melt, allowing it to drip down the sides of the glass. Divide the drink evenly among the glasses. Garnish each drink with a gummy worm. Elixir mixer!

Pumpkin Pie CONES

Playing among the pine trees in the North Pole forest gave us an easy-as-pie idea that's filled with spice and sweetness, just right for your Thanksgiving celebration. Aren't you grateful we substituted pumpkin for the pine cones, though? Whew. The pine was too ewwy-chewy! (P.S. We're grateful for YOU.)

FOR THE PIE FILLING

- One 0.25-ounce envelope unflavored gelatin powder (see Sweet Shop Secret below)
- One 3.9-ounce box instant vanilla pudding and pie filling
- 2 cups whole milk
- 1 cup pumpkin puree (not pie filling)
- 2 teaspoons pumpkin pie spice
- ½ cup sugar
- 1 cup whipped topping

FOR THE PIE CONES

- 6 ounces orange candy melts
- 8 to 10 sugar cones (#310 size), such as Joy brand
- Fall-themed festive sprinkles
- 10 gingersnap cookies or 4 full-sheet graham crackers, finely crushed (about ½ cup)

SPECIAL EQUIPMENT
Pastry bag fitted with large round tip

1. Make the pie filling: Add the gelatin powder to 1 cup warm water and whisk until completely dissolved. Set aside.
2. In a large bowl, whisk together the pudding and milk until thickened, about 2 minutes. Add the bloomed gelatin and whisk to combine. Add the pumpkin puree, pumpkin pie spice, and sugar and whisk until creamy. Add the whipped topping and continue whisking until light and fluffy, about 3 minutes.
3. Refrigerate the mixture for at least 6 hours or up to overnight.
4. Decorate and fill the cones: Line a sheet pan with parchment paper and set aside.
5. Place the melts in a microwave-safe bowl. Microwave on high, uncovered, in 30-second increments, stirring in between, until melted and smooth.
6. Dip the cones in the candy melt to coat the outer edges by 1 inch. Coat the dipped area with sprinkles and set aside on the prepared sheet pan to harden, about 10 minutes.
7. Place about 1 tablespoon of cookie crumbs in the bottom of each cone. Fill the pastry bag with pie filling and fill each cone with about ⅓ cup of pie filling for a pumpkin pie cone treat!

SWEET SHOP SECRET
Dissolving gelatin powder in warm water, or "blooming," ensures a smooth, clump-free, no-bake pie filling that will be easy to pipe into your pie cones!

SURPRISE SNACK MIX-UP

**MAKES 4 CUPS
SNACK MIX**

We know you know your ABCs. Rearrange the first letter of each ingredient to spell out what kind of snack we mixed up for you to bring to school!

- ☐ ½ cup **A**lmonds
- ☐ ½ cup **D**ried apples
- ☐ ½ cup **H**oney nut cereal O's
- ☐ ½ cup **S**alted mini pretzels
- ☐ ½ cup **S**unflower seeds
- ☐ ½ cup **Y**ogurt-covered raisins
- ☐ ¼ cup **C**hocolate chips
- ☐ ¼ cup **L**etter cookies
- ☐ ¼ cup **O**range jelly beans
- ☐ ¼ cup **O**reo cookie minis

1. Place all the ingredients in a large bowl and mix well to combine. Transfer to an airtight container and store at room temperature for up to 2 weeks.
2. Portion in a snack bag and bring to school!

(Answer: "School Days" Snack Mix)

We ♥ You STRAWBERRY MILKSHAKE

MAKES 1 MILKSHAKE, PLUS A BIT EXTRA FOR A MINI MILKSHAKE

We're having a Scout Elf heart-to-heart convo and think the best way to show our love for you this Valentine's Day is with a sweet treat for sharing—with us, of course! Here is everything you need to make us a strawberry-swirled, whipped cream-twirled, decked-out Sweet Shop-style shake. We ♥ you!

- ☐ ¼ cup strawberry buttercream (see page 9) or store-bought frosting
- ☐ ¼ cup candy conversation hearts
- ☐ 12 or more Elf-Size Doughnut Delights! (page 55), iced and covered with red and white sprinkles
- ☐ Red and white sprinkles
- ☐ 1½ cups strawberry ice cream
- ☐ ½ cup whole milk
- ☐ 6 strawberries, hulled and halved
- ☐ Whipped topping
- ☐ 1 tablespoon strawberry syrup
- ☐ 1 store-bought heart-shaped sugar cookie
- ☐ Maraschino cherry

SPECIAL EQUIPMENT
One 12- to 16-ounce milkshake glass, tall glass, or pint glass

Blender

Drinking straw

1. Use a butter knife to spread a thick coating of buttercream on the rim and about 2 inches around the top of the outside of the milkshake glass.

2. Press the candy hearts and doughnuts into the frosting—it will act as glue. Cover any open spaces with sprinkles. Place the glass in the freezer for 10 minutes.

3. Meanwhile, make the milkshake. In the blender, combine the ice cream, milk, and strawberries. Blend on high speed until smooth. Remove the glass from the freezer and pour in the milkshake. Top with whipped topping, strawberry syrup, the cookie, and the cherry and add the straw.

4. Reserve the remaining milkshake to make a Scout Elf Mini Milkshake! (see Sweet Shop Secret below). Let's have a heart-to-heart convo about how much we ♥ being back for Valentine's Day!

SWEET SHOP SECRET
Mini Milkshake!

Decorate a 1.5- to 2-ounce cordial or shot glass rim and top with a smidge of frosting and sprinkles. Fill the glass with a bit of the strawberry milkshake and top with whipped topping, syrup, cherry, and a candy heart. Cut a drinking straw in thirds for an elf-size straw.

Loading Christmas Spirit...

Sweet Shop Elves
INTERVIEW

Now that we've whisked our way through the holiday season, we're ready to reveal some of our favorites. Do you agree with our choices? (P.S. Which Sweet Shop Elf is your favorite?)

PICKLES MCCHEER

Favorite Recipe: Bitty Burger Bites
Favorite Kitchen Gadget: Blender
Favorite Magical Ingredient: Pickle juice
Fun Fact: Pickles' favorite breakfast is . . . a pickle smoothie!

GINGER JINGLEBOOTS

Favorite Recipe: We ♥ You
Strawberry Milkshake
Favorite Kitchen Gadget: Spatula
Favorite Magical Ingredient: Sprinkles
Fun Fact: Ginger loves the Sweet Shop, but she also helps Mrs. Claus design elf shoes!

Nice boots!

TOFFEE TINSELTON

Favorite Recipe: Petite sweetzas
Favorite Kitchen Gadget: Whisk
Favorite Magical Ingredient: Brown sugar
Fun Fact: Toffee's favorite Christmas song is "Deck the Halls."

DASH O'JOLLY

Favorite Recipe: Snow Blizzard Cream
Favorite Kitchen Gadget: Ice cream maker
Favorite Magical Ingredient: Snow!
Fun Fact: Dash is a former three-time champion North Pole Snowballer!

Bonus:
SCOUT ELF SNAFUS

> I don't know for sure, but I think the humans hit a glitch or two and need our advice!

> What happened?

YOUR SCOUT ELF HASN'T ARRIVED YET

- They're doing a bit of sightseeing first with a Scout Elf friend assigned to another country! They may even bring back a recipe or idea to share—Bûche de Noël Nibbles!, anyone?

- They're still completing the North Pole tasks that Santa gave them before leaving. Patience!

- Santa extended Scout Elf training to make sure they're in top shape!

- A snowstorm was brewing at the North Pole and they had to wait to travel safely.

- They had too many treats at the Sweet Shop and they needed a few extra days to digest.

> We're always prepared to help!

> Here are some Scout Elf mishap scenarios and solutions.

YOUR ELF HASN'T MOVED!

- Your Scout Elf returned to their favorite spot! You have yours in your house, right?

- They're waiting to cook/bake/watch a Christmas movie again! Same spot, different day.

- Santa gave them a very time-consuming duty on their nightly trip back to the North Pole, leaving little time to create a new spot when they returned.

- It's the cookies and sweets! Again! It's no wonder they haven't moved. They're full!

- They heard someone coming, quickly picked a spot, and what do you know? Same one!

- They did move—take a closer look! Can't you see the slight change? They sometimes test your observation skills.

- Someone touched them, resulting in their loss of magic, and they're trying to tell you by showing how weary they are! (I know, we saved the worst for last.) But read below right now!

Oh, look . . . they're smiling.

We hope this helped!

IF AN ELFTASTROPHE OCCURS!!

When a human accidentally or deliberately touches an Elf on the Shelf, it results in a sudden loss of Christmas magic. Luckily, there are three remedies—but you must promise not to overuse them!

1. Write a letter of apology and send it to Santa fast! Leave it with your Scout Elves. They'll muster up enough magic to get themselves to the North Pole ER for recovery and a cup of cocoa . . . STAT!
2. Sprinkle a touch of cinnamon near your elf to revive them—it's like a vitamin for elves!
3. Sing a Christmas carol, at full volume, with joy in your heart!

Fast Feats of FESTIVE FUN

ACKNOWLEDGMENTS

In my family, sharing meals and baking—especially at Christmastime—is a time-honored tradition. We have an annual cookie decorating contest, cookie exchanges, and festive holiday treats to prepare and give as gifts. So it seemed fitting that we, as the family who first shared The Elf on the Shelf with you, combine our two favorite holiday traditions into a cookbook fit for elves and elf helpers everywhere to enjoy. As Santa's Chief Storyteller, I'm so pleased to help Mrs. Claus' special crew of Sweet Shop Elves bring some sweetness and spice to your holiday celebrations. Hopefully, their ideas will inspire your own Scout Elves to new and exciting edible creations.

Of course, Santa and Mrs. Claus brought a whole crew together to deliver these recipes, games, activities, and fun from the North Pole to you. I'm so grateful to each dedicated contributor for the beauty and joy they brought to this book. We hope it brings you good cheer and lots of Christmas magic for many years to come!

—Chanda A. Bell

WOW! So many talented North Pole helpers!

WILLIAM MORROW

Vice President/Editorial Director: Cassie Jones
Assistant Editor: Jill Zimmerman
Senior Designer: Jennifer Chung
Designer: Paul Miele-Herndon
Senior Production Editor: Shelby Peak
Associate Director, Production: Anna Brower
Publicity Manager: Emily Dansky
Senior Marketing Director: Melissa Esner

COLLABORATORS

Recipe Creator/Co-Writer: Theresa Gambacorta
Recipe Assistants: Amy Donato, Jeanette Fletcher

Food Stylist: Katelyn Hardwick
Food Stylist Assistants: Phillip Meeker, Lauren Gildea, Lulu Gyoury

Photographer: Genya O'Neall
Photography Assistant: Aarion Joseph
DigiTech: Scarlett Fulbright

Modeling Agency: C2 Kids (Atlanta)
Model Agent: Carrie Allen
Models: Jaxon James, Harper Housley, Baylor Davis, Larson Hamby, Armando Orellana, Toan Clarke, Carys Varner, Brylie Burkett, Merritt Stephens
Hair/Makeup: Jenna Atkins
Child Labor Coordinator: Andrea Brown

THE LUMISTELLA COMPANY

Senior Vice President, Creative: Andrea Esposito
Art Direction and Design: Laura Berkeley
Editor/Story Lead: Kristy Dempsey
Support Team: Mike Marano, Rami Callahan, Courtney Lulkin, Kaeti MacNeil, Allison Roberts, Tanya Seale, Madison Sosebee, Jen Clements, Paul Eulette, Emilie Bauer

universal
CONVERSION CHART

OVEN TEMPERATURE EQUIVALENTS

250°F = 120°C
275°F = 135°C
300°F = 150°C
325°F = 160°C
350°F = 180°C
375°F = 190°C
400°F = 200°C
425°F = 220°C
450°F = 230°C
475°F = 240°C
500°F = 260°C

MEASUREMENT EQUIVALENTS

Measurements should always be level unless directed otherwise.

⅛ teaspoon = 0.5 mL
¼ teaspoon = 1 mL
½ teaspoon = 2 mL
1 teaspoon = 5 mL
1 tablespoon = 3 teaspoons = ½ fluid ounce = 15 mL
2 tablespoons = ⅛ cup = 1 fluid ounce = 30 mL
4 tablespoons = ¼ cup = 2 fluid ounces = 60 mL
5⅓ tablespoons = ⅓ cup = 3 fluid ounces = 80 mL
8 tablespoons = ½ cup = 4 fluid ounces = 120 mL
10⅔ tablespoons = ⅔ cup = 5 fluid ounces = 160 mL
12 tablespoons = ¾ cup = 6 fluid ounces = 180 mL
16 tablespoons = 1 cup = 8 fluid ounces = 240 mL

INDEX

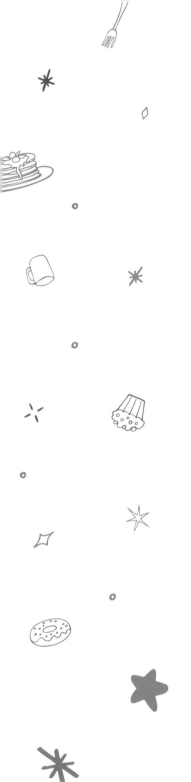

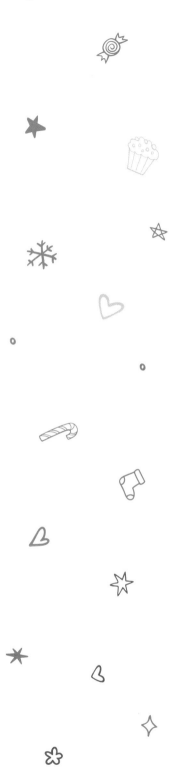

our Favorite
RECIPES

Favorite
SCOUT ELF MOMENTS

HarperCollins books may be purchased for educational, business, or sales promotional use. For information, please email the Special Markets Department at SPsales@harpercollins.com.

FIRST EDITION

Photographs © 2024 The Lumistella Company
Chapter 5 opener map © Zhuko/stock.adobe.com
Emojis © Cali6ro/stock.adobe.com
Pages 154–155 flags © R. Gino Santa Maria/stock.adobe.com, filipbjorkman/stock.adobe.com, Archer7/stock.adobe.com, aomvector/stock.adobe.com, 12ee12/stock.adobe.com, Tarik GOK/stock.adobe.com, G7 Stock/stock.adobe.com, and Cobalt/stock.adobe.com
Miscellaneous doodles and line drawings © Shutterstock

Library of Congress Cataloging-in-Publication Data

Names: Bell, Chanda A., author. | O'Neall, Genya, photographer.

Title: The elf on the shelf family cookbook : 50 elftastic recipes, plus playful elf ideas, games, activities, and more! / by Chanda A. Bell ; photography by Genya O'Neall.

Description: First edition. | New York, NY : William Morrow, 2024. | Includes index. | Summary: "A full-color, gifty Christmas cookbook filled with recipes, activities, and holiday magic, guided by the brand's signature Scout Elves"—Provided by publisher.

Identifiers: LCCN 2024011605 (print) | LCCN 2024011606 (ebook) | ISBN 9780063345737 (hardcover) | ISBN 9780063345744 (ebook)

Subjects: LCSH: Christmas cooking. | Amusements. | Cooking for Children. | Elves—Miscellanea. | LCGFT: Cookbooks.

Classification: LCC TX739.2.C45 B455 2024 (print) | LCC TX739.2.C45 (ebook) | DDC 641.5/686—dc23/eng/20240410

LC record available at https://lccn.loc.gov/2024011605

LC ebook record available at https://lccn.loc.gov/2024011606

ISBN 978-0-06-334573-7

24 25 26 27 28 LBC 5 4 3 2 1